U

Copyright © 1986 by

University Press of America,® Inc.

4720 Boston Way
Lanham, MD 20706

3 Henrietta Street
London WC2E 8LU England

Library of Congress Cataloging in Publication Data

Von Blum, Paul.
    Stillborn education.

    Bibliography: p.
    Includes index.
    1. Universities and colleges—United States—
Graduate work.   2. Research institutes—United States.
3. Universities and colleges—United States—
Departments.   4. Interdisciplinary approach in
education.—United States.   5. University of California,
Los Angeles—Graduate work—Case studies.   I. Title.
LB2371.V66   1986   378'.1553'0973   86-13215
ISBN 0-8191-5509-8 (alk. paper)
ISBN 0-8191-5510-1 (pbk. : alk. paper)

All University Press of America books are produced on acid-free
paper which exceeds the minimum standards set by the National
Historical Publications and Records Commission.

to Ruth and Elizabeth

ACKNOWLEDGEMENTS

Writing the acknowledgements for a book is a double source of satisfaction. Above all, it is deeply gratifying to thank the many people who bring genuine meaning to the notion of collaboration. And the acknowledgements are the final thing that remains before the manuscript, at long last, is completed. Most authors know that particular mixture of joy and relief.

Various friends and colleagues have made such significant contributions that no words of gratitude could possibly be adequate. Professor Paul Rosenthal of the UCLA Communication Studies Program has discussed higher education with me for more than six years. In our scores of conversations, he has revealed an extraordinary ability to identify the central defects of modern academic life. That critical perspective fundamentally informs the present book. I would only add that if most academics shared his vision of undergraduate education and emulated his unshakable personal integrity, there would be little need for a book like STILLBORN EDUCATION. Professor Fred Reif of the UC Berkeley Physics Department has been similarly influential. Our educational discussions have taken place regularly since the late '60's. Both his specific criticisms of university priorities and organization and his general analytic rigor have been profoundly valuable to me. Although this book is probably not quite what he might have expected, I hope the differences are matters of personal temperament and style. I must also acknowledge a long intellectual debt to Professor James E. Harmon, who first showed me how to look beneath the seductive official rhetoric of major social institutions. His own experiences as a university faculty member and administrator helped me to more fully understand the problems of higher education.

Marde Gregory of the UCLA Speech Department has been extremely helpful during the life of this project. Her personal encouragement and her tireless and difficult attempts to bring educational decency to the University of California have fortified my will to complete this book. Scott Cooper has been a tremendous source of personal and intellectual support.

Beyond his substantial contributions to my specific arguments, Scott has convinced me again that the life of an academic dissenter is a life worth living -- partly because it generates and sustains relationships with people of his quality. Precisely the same comments need to be said about Barbara Sackoff Lampert. Her specific advice on social science methodology has been invaluable, but not nearly as much as her friendship and support. Karin Pally too has contributed valuable insights about academic life. But her personal friendship and support for this kind of project are even more meaningful to me. Joan McDowell, formerly administrative assistant in the UCLA Program in Medicine, Law, and Human Values, has similarly been committed to my vision of undergraduate teaching. Her perceptive comments about education have also proved valuable to me in this book. I want to mention my deep gratitude to Assemblyman John Vasconcellos of the California State Legislature. His career-long commitment to working for humane higher education in California has been inspirational to me -- a term I have never used until now. Moreover, John has closely followed my own struggles with sympathy and compassion. We desperately need more political leaders like him.

I have been fortunate to have discussed higher education with several faculty colleagues at the University of California and elsewhere over the years. Many of these people were unaware that our conversations might inform a future book -- and neither was I for much of the time. It is extremely important to mention that I name these individuals because I want to express my thanks to them. It implies absolutely nothing about their agreement or disagreement with the views expressed in this book: Bill Winslade, Bernard Towers, Judy Ross, John Schacher, Brad Burns, Hal Borko, Al Boime, Jeff Cole, Geoff Cowan, Lisa Gerrard, Tom Miller, Clarence Lo, Carole Fabricant, Gerry Cavanaugh, Jeff Lustig, Alain Renoir, Alan Schoenfeld, Laura Reif, Dick Jacobs, Tom Elliot, Don Castro, Jay Bregman, and Preston Covey.

Probably my most sustained source of stimulations comes from my students. Without doubt, my contact with bright, responsive, and critical undergraduates has been the highlight of my professional life. This book would not be possible without their assistance. Conversations about higher education with the following former and present students have had value for me far beyond what they may have ever realized: Ellen Clark, John Trochet, Linda DeSitter, Vic Lieberman, Robbie Lieberman, Marty Rutherford, DeeDee Dickey, Claire Baker, Laurence Hall, Stewart Wachs, Lori Teller, Lois Kochan, David Sheff, Mard Naman, Eleanor Walden, Don Margolis, Kathy Keilch, Steve Faber, John Morgan, Wendy Jaeger, Steve Pantilat, Tony Steimle, Dina Seredian, Valerie Kincaid, Randy Kincaid, Karen Streicher, Helene Wasserman, Tim Fulkerson, John Hotta, Suzy Smith, Gwyn Lurie, Robyn Roth, Natalie Hale, Julane Marx, Steve Blum, Sandy Slater, Paul Arshagouni, Randi Shafton, Adam Dodd, Julie Riekes, Ken Morrison, Erika Silver, and Carlos Perez. Many have become close friends, probably the biggest personal benefit of university teaching. I know there must be some unconscionable omissions, which I deeply regret.

I would be remiss if I neglected various other personal friends who have encouraged me to continue, even in the most troubling moments of struggle and doubt: Steve Ferrey, Ben Kaplan, Judith Shafton-Kaplan, Edie Harmon, Hans van Marle, Antje deWilde, John Bergman, Aaron Lansky, Michael Cohen, Gerald Rise, Gerry Graber, Jane Schoenfeld, Charlie Manske, Dawn Motyka, Ron Goldstein, Sally Goldstein, Doc Berry, and Carol Berne. My parents, Peter and Selma Von Blum, continually provided similar support.

Ruth Von Blum was once again my most important collaborator. She has, as usual, been involved in every stage of the project, from initial conception to final execution. She has gone over every word of the manuscript and made analytic and editorial corrections that I was far too blind or bull-headed to do myself. These contributions would be monumental in themselves. But they are augmented by her love and support, in good times and in stressful times. Her love has been a powerful stimulus during this project, and not only because of the inevitable mishegoss of writing a book. She has been profoundly behind my political struggles to implement my educational vision. She has comforted me when I have felt like Joseph K. in THE TRIAL. And she has shared my rage at those bureaucrats who have forgotten what a university is really supposed to be. Most important, she has made me remember that a loving personal relationship and family life are far more valuable than a "successful" academic career.

TABLE OF CONTENTS

PREFACE

A book preface permits the author many liberties that would be awkward in the text itself. It encourages a form of personal expression that reveals the motivations behind the project. I am therefore eager to provide a personal overview to show why, despite my other books and academic activities, this is my most important effort--one, in fact, in process for more than twenty years.

In the Introductory chapter, I note my seventeen years of teaching at the University of California as background to my participant/observer methodology. For most of that time, through both circumstance and design, I have been an academic maverick operating on the periphery of university life. My passion for educational criticism and reform, however, predates my faculty service. As a participant in the now famous Free Speech Movement, I was concerned, like thousands of my fellow students, about the educational problems on the Berkeley campus. We were angry at the low priority of undergraduate education there (and by implication at other large and prestigious universities). We were disturbed by the way knowledge was presented in absurdly narrow and fragmented packages. Above all, I shared the widespread belief that the organization of learning into minute academic fields worked powerfully against the goal of a genuinely liberal and critical education.

These beliefs led me to work personally to implement my educational vision. My introduction to university life began in earnest in 1968 when I joined the faculty of the Department of Rhetoric at Berkeley. It became quickly apparent that my youthful ideals would clash dramatically with institutional realities. After my first year of teaching, a senior member of the Department called me into his office for a candid conversation. Remarking that my teaching record was commendable, he nevertheless undertook to inform me about life in a high-powered university. He spoke sincerely and with obvious interest in my personal academic future. He sought to provide advice that would facilitate my advancement within accepted channels at the University of California. In this conversation, he made a remark that has had a profound effect upon me ever since: "Paul, we don't give a shit about teaching." He went on to indicate that teaching excellence barely counts when it comes to promotion. Shaken, I knew that my path at Berkeley would hardly be smooth. It is worth adding that in a conversation shortly before this book went to press, a Department Chairperson at another University of California campus reiterated the point. He mentioned that in his sixteen years of service, he had never known any faculty member on his campus to be promoted for educational contributions or teaching alone.

In 1972, the Rhetoric Department declined to renew my faculty appointment for the following academic year. By then, I had achieved some recognition as a teacher among Berkeley undergraduates. My dismissal generated a minor campus-wide controversy, culminating in my appointment for the next year to the recently created Division of Interdisciplinary and General Studies (DIGS).

DIGS was my first experience with a marginal, interdisciplinary academic program. Very quickly, this program, with its exclusive emphasis on undergraduate education, became a cause celebre on campus. As head of the social science field major, the largest unit within DIGS, I became a key participant in the public controversy, struggling together with my colleagues and students for the preservation of the program. An analysis of the controversy, and of its broader implications for the prospects of institutional reform, appears in Chapter 7.

In 1977 and 1978, after the controversy widened beyond the Berkeley campus, I testified before a committee of the California State Assembly on the specific problems of the Division of Interdisciplinary and General Studies and the more fundamental educational inadequacies of the University of California. Throughout these years, I became increasingly visible as an outspoken critic of contemporary university affairs. This perspective informs the present book.

In 1979, I resigned my faculty position at Berkeley. After a brief break in service, I rejoined the staff of the University of California in 1980, this time at UCLA in the capacity of academic administrator and faculty member. Again, I attempted to guide interdisciplinary alternatives to the standard university fare, especially the Freshman/Sophomore

Professional School Seminar Program (also discussed in Chapter 7). And again, I have been vocal in criticizing university priorities and calling attention to the deplorable state of undergraduate education.

I have thus been a strong advocate of interdisciplinary activity and of a higher status for undergraduate education in the American research university. As an active partisan in matters of higher education, I seek to promote awareness about university defects among my fellow academics and the broader public. Although I have no desire to eliminate academic disciplines or denigrate legitimate research, I believe that present priorities are severely out of balance and that research universities are insufficiently accountable to their students and to the public.

In each of my previous books, I have deliberately noted that I stand apart from the supposedly "value-free" perspective of social inquiry. Never more than in this present work have I felt so strongly about that stance. The human stakes are too high to pretend to be detached from the moral and political battles of our times.

Venice, California
April, 1986

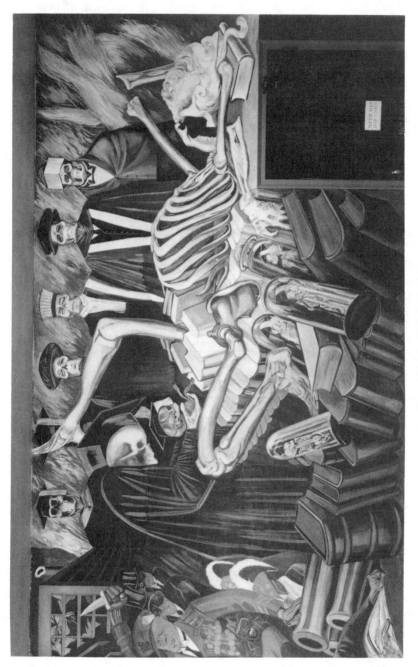

Jose Clemente Orozco, (1883-1949), Mexican
The Epic of American Civilization, Panel # 17, Gods of the Modern World.
Fresco, 1932-1934.   P.934.13.17
Courtesy of the Trustees of Dartmouth College, Hanover, N.H.

CHAPTER 1

Introduction: The Misguided Multiversity

In late 1982 and early 1983, the Conference Board of the Associated Research Council released its ratings of doctoral programs in universities throughout the United States. Eagerly awaited by faculty members and administrators, these rankings are enormously important in creating and fortifying university reputations as well as indirectly fostering the personal careers of professors in highly rated academic departments. The 1982/83 results were predictable. Such academic giants as Harvard, Yale, UC Berkeley, Stanford, M.I.T., and others topped the lists in various academic fields. Other universities, with some of their individual departments listed in the top ten, felt an increased sense of institutional status and prestige.

The reaction at UCLA was both typical and revealing. Although none of its departmental doctoral programs was rated Number one, most of its programs in the arts and sciences did extremely well. Its overall ranking, in fact, was Number five in the entire country. This meant that the professors who evaluated graduate programs throughout the United States viewed UCLA as a premier center for academic research, the foundation for Ph.D. level instruction in contemporary higher education. The release of these rankings deeply gratified UCLA faculty members, administrators, and other officials. The public relations apparatus of the campus mobilized to take advantage of the newly official academic standing of the University of California at Los Angeles.

More important, for more than three years, UCLA has been proclaiming its status as the fifth ranking American university to itself and the general public. I have read several internal documents that boldly assert that UCLA is number five in the nation. This is done without qualifying the rating by

1

explaining that it referred only to its doctoral programs in arts and sciences. Increasingly, people throughout the campus have accepted the number five graduate ranking as synonymous with overall institutional excellence. Administrators, faculty, staff, and students have uncritically assumed that there are only four superior institutions of higher learning in the country.

This deceptive image has been promoted regularly and deliberately. An official of the UCLA public relations office told me candidly that the objective is to get the public to perceive UCLA as the fifth best university in America. She noted that the fact that this ranking related solely to doctoral programs was underplayed or even ignored in various communications. Similarly, university authorities have used this approach to attract the finest high school students. In publications and oral presentations, UCLA personnel have informed prospective students that they could enroll in one of the top five schools in America. This impression has had its intended effect. Students in large numbers have come to believe that their education as undergraduates is of front-rank quality. In Southern California, the general public, largely indifferent to such matters, has little reason to disbelieve the public relations claims of UCLA.

The smugness and dishonesty that have characterized UCLA's response to the Associated Research Council's rankings are, in microcosm, what is wrong with much of academic life today. Privately, many UCLA officials know well that these ratings reflect no more than a distanced judgment of faculty peers throughout the nation. Indeed, they are aware that such judgments are based exclusively on the research stature of professors within specific academic disciplines. They know too that these evaluations often reflect little more than perceived visibility within narrow scholarly circles.

Most significant, despite their rhetoric to the contrary, many UCLA administrators and professors realize that there is no necessary connection between research recognition and daily educational quality. They understand that there is no automatic relationship between what a professor publishes in an academic journal and what he or she is able to do with undergraduate students in the classroom or office. In candid moments, they sometimes admit that graduate rankings are

2

useless as a guide to the nature and quality of undergraduate instruction. In one particularly honest conversation with a senior UCLA administrator, I was told that the emphasis on graduate rankings was not only misleading, but that for many professors, there is an inverse relationship between their research stature and their qualities as undergraduate educators.

There are probably hundreds of schools where bright undergraduates can find a far superior educational atmosphere than they can obtain at UCLA or scores of similar research universities. Colleges such as Swarthmore, Williams, Smith, Haverford, Pomona, and numerous others offer undergraduate students the kind of close interaction with first-rate professors that is exceedingly rare in large research institutions. Young men and women seeking a genuine liberal arts education can find many better prospects than most of the universities winning accolades from the Associated Research Council.

The intentional manipulation of narrowly based graduate rankings--itself a highly arbitrary process--in order to elevate general university recognition is a sign of the misguided, antieducational priorities that dominate most research universities in modern America. The blunt reality is that education in general and undergraduate education in particular are at best marginal concerns. The quest, indeed the obsession, for national rankings have obscured the historic mission of providing a broad, critical education for hundreds of thousands of students attending large research universities.

That nationally known institutions have severely neglected such an important function is scarcely known by the general public. Taxpayers who support public universities generally have little idea how their money is really spent. This situation exists because the problems of higher education typically evoke minimal interest from the mass media. Only when the massive political explosions of the 1960's and 1970's occurred did the press and television deal, however superficially, with the underlying problems of education in large research universities. Furthermore, all organizations interpret and disseminate information in order to maximize self-interest and reputation. Universities are thus reluctant to promote anything other than an idealized version of their internal values and operations. Even academic officials who are privately critical of the gap between public rhetoric and daily educational reality are reticent, in understandable fear of career and personal consequences. This phenomenon, of course, is hardly confined to higher education. Hospitals, law enforcement agencies, corporations, the media, the professions, and others seek to promote only the most favorable public image and to deflect attention from their inadequacies.

It is time for a more critical analysis of this reality. The self-congratulatory posture of UCLA during the past few years reflects attitudes found widely throughout the world of prestigious research universities in America. The comments and criticisms in this book are intended to apply to scores of institutions besides the University of California. Their major personnel at both faculty and administrative levels share common backgrounds, training, and professional values and aspirations. Predominantly upper middle class careerists, they have embraced traditional American notions of success. It is thus no accident that academic discourse and behavior are virtually identical in Westwood, Berkeley, Ann Arbor, Madison, Cambridge, Chapel Hill, and elsewhere. Local differences pale in comparison to the dominant ideology of high academic visibility in specialized scholarly disciplines.

The critical view espoused in this book is hardly the expression of a few student discontents. In 1985, several national reports indicated a major educational crisis in American universities. Although differing in scope and emphasis, reports from the National Institute of Education ("Involvement in Learning: Realizing the Potential of American Higher Education"), the Association of American Colleges ("Integrity in the College Curriculum: A Report to the Academic Community"), and the National Endowment for the Humanities ("To Reclaim a Legacy"), reveal severe problems in contemporary higher education. Among other criticisms, these reports contend that effective teaching occupies an increasingly lower priority in American colleges and universities. Both institutions and individual faculty members, they claim, care more about status and academic reputation than about the educational needs of their students. Above all, they argue that this educational neglect will have catastrophic consequences for students facing the challenges of the coming century.

4

My personal academic experiences persuade me that the recent national criticism is both accurate and understated. My background includes 17 years of faculty and administrative service at four branches of the University of California, the bulk of which involved teaching at its two most dominant campuses, Berkeley and UCLA. I have taught in several humanities and social science departments, some traditional and some experimental. My overall critique stems from the perspective of a marginal insider. Beyond my teaching, I have also served as an administrator for the National Endowment for the Humanities and as an educational consultant and evaluator. This work has combined with my own scholarly interests to permit me to visit major research campuses and hold conversations with hundreds of students, professors, and administrators. What follows, then, is a series of observations and reflections based on my extensive work in the academic world.

My method is simply to report reality as I have come to perceive it. This approach is deeply informed by three related traditions of social inquiry in the United States. The first is the participant/observer perspective associated with qualitative social science. Operating within the spirit of this methodology, I have engaged in firsthand observation over a substantial period of time. During my years as an academic, I have sought to understand the major actors in a complex social world and to obtain information through direct experience in that setting. Daily immersion in the multifaceted activities of major research universities has generated an insider's sense of institutional values and practices. These are the elements that form the culture of all organizations.[1]

This book is equally influenced by the critical tradition in modern scholarship and journalism. For many decades, there have been social analysts who have rejected the ideology of supposedly "value-free," "objective" social science. They have combined their investigations with clear statements of their own desires for major social and political change. Eschewing neutrality, they have presented their intellectual work as intrinsic to their broader commitment to eliminating the oppressive conditions and institutions they identify and analyze in their publications.[2]

One strain of this critical tradition has especially informed the present work. Virtually all institutions and professions have

5

dissenting voices who decline, for various reasons, to adhere to the prevailing orthodoxy. These dissenters find themselves in institutions whose values and priorities appear to distort the original goals that attracted them in the first place. Some of these dissidents find it impossible to remain silent and have grown frustrated with the usual internal mechanisms to offer criticism and promote change. In the process, they have created a substantial body of critical literature calling public attention to internal professional defects. The present effort attempts to augment that tradition.[3]

Finally, this book is hardly the first major critique of the dominant institutions of higher learning. In Europe and America, there is an intellectually dynamic tradition of educational criticism. For many years, critics of universities have called attention to virtually every defective feature of academic existence. In recent times, the social ferment of the 1960's generated impressive additions to that tradition. Many observers wrote persuasively about such issues as the complicity of universities in the cold war; racial and sexual discrimination in higher education; corporate control of university governance and operations; the manipulation of academic research for inappropriate and oppressive social, economic, and political objectives; the estrangement of academic knowledge from the profound moral and social problems of the 20th century; and many other inadequacies of contemporary academic affairs. I am sympathetic with the overwhelming majority of these efforts. The present work, however, will complement these powerful criticisms by emphasizing the educational deficiencies of the modern university, particularly relating to the needs of undergraudate students. This book therefore adds one more dimension to the much broader tradition of educational dissent.[4]

My extensive observations of highly regarded research universities lead me to some distressing conclusions. As a preface to my critique, I should note that there is also much that is desirable about this institution. Despite the glaring failures that will be the central focus of this book, fairness requires the judgment that the modern university has made some profound and durable contributions to society. It has, for example, provided at times an organizational base for the preservation of intellectual freedom. The university has generally been tolerant of persons of diverse social and political ideologies. Many people with unorthodox ideas have been able to survive in universities even if they have been unable to prosper. Significantly, their freedom to develop and experiment with unpopular ideas probably could not have been possible in other institutional settings. Neither government nor industry is inclined to support the broad range of intellectual work found in university settings. Moreover, alternative institutions such as independent think tanks are marginal at best, providing support for a mere handful of creative thinkers, scholars, and social critics. Clearly, intellectual curiosity is best served in traditional institutions of higher learning in America.

No one, furthermore, can can deny the stature of at least some of the research produced in America universities. Particularly in the sciences, the accomplishments have often been spectacular, with thousands of positive applications for human beings. Research in medicine and other health sciences, of course, has been an important contribution from universities throughout the land. Other areas of research, though less visible in terms of public impact, have also been valuable additions to human knowledge and understanding.

The modern research university has also made some important educational contributions. Despite the present imbalance of priorities, there are thousands of faculty members in American universities for whom teaching is a high personal priority. For these men and women, close contact with undergraduate students is professionally gratifying. As teachers, they do much more than merely provide information to passive student audiences. Rather, they stimulate students to think critically and to develop an intellectual framework that will serve them in all facets of their lives. These professors represent the highest ideals of the academic profession.

These positive accomplishments have unfortunately been muted by the wide and increasing gap between academic potential and academic practice. It is time to go beyond the pleasant but misleading rhetoric of university catalogues and similar publications. Instead, it is necessary to explore the defects of academic life thoroughly and systematically.

What, then, are the present problems of modern universities that are ordinarily hidden from public view and scrutiny? The answer requires an historical perspective. Developments

7

during the past three decades have had profound and generally negative consequences for the academic world in the United States.

The research-oriented university has played a dominant role in American higher education since World War II. The proliferation of extramural funding from government agencies, foundations, and corporations has transformed the very character of the university as an institution. It has strengthened research priorities and has contributed to the decline of undergraduate general education. The widespread availability of money naturally stimulated thousands of professors to move in directions that would augment their incomes and reputations. Over the years, this movement has been institutionalized in the form of a misplaced scheme of values that has made life for undergraduates precarious and unrewarding.

While many academics were delighted with a system that provided professional status for narrow research production, others realized that this priority, if taken to excess, could result in widespread student dissatisfaction. Even before the tumultuous events of the 1960's, many internal observers saw that universities were becoming blind to some major educational problems.

One of the most astute observers was Clark Kerr, the former President of the University of California. Even as he served as one of the primary architects of the post-war research university, he understood that success could be costly. In his remarkably perceptive book, *The Uses of the University*, written revealingly only a short time before the student protests at Berkeley and elsewhere, Kerr identified many of the educational difficulties of the post-war university:

> [T]here are some problems to be fully faced, and they are problems of consequence.
>
> One is the improvement of undergraduate instruction in the university. It will require the solution to many sub-problems: how to give adequate recognition to the teaching skill as well as to the research performance of the faculty; how to create a curriculum that serves the needs of the students as well as the research interests of the teacher; how to prepare the generalist as well as

the specialist in an age of specialization . . .; how to treat the individual student as a unique human being in the mass student body; . . . how to establish a range of contact between faculty and students broader than the one-way route across the lectern or through the television screen; how to raise educational policy once again to the forefront of faculty concerns.[5]

Unfortunately, Kerr's interest in undergraduate education was more theoretical than actual. His presidency of the University of California coincided with the time that that institution evolved into a large research and entrepreneurial entity concerned more with money and status than with the intellectual needs of undergraduates. His seminal book, in fact, is the best description of and apology for the post-war changes in academic structure and priorities.

A closer scrutiny of *The Uses of the University* is a valuable preface to a more systematic critique of the modern university. Kerr coined the now familiar term "multiversity" to describe this new pluralist organization that would provide something for everyone in its mandate to produce knowledge for society. Kerr's multiversity would be a social service station that would respond to the demands of the government and the dominant interests of the economy:

Knowledge is now central to society. It is wanted, even demanded, by more people and more institutions than ever before. The university as producer, wholesaler, and retailer of knowledge cannot escape service. Knowledge, today, is for everybody's sake.[6]

When he wrote this more than twenty years ago, he knew well that the total integration of the research university into the political and economic fabric of society *would* have permanent implications for education. The vast infusion of research funds altered virtually everything in university life, including the attitudes and even the personalities of faculty members, administrators, and students. Since the creation of new knowledge was now the central objective, other functions would have to assume a subordinate status. Ever candid, Dr. Kerr perceptively chronicled the results:

9

The reasons for the general deterioration of undergraduate teaching are several. Teaching loads and student contact hours have been reduced. Faculty members are more frequently on leave or temporarily away from campus. More of the instruction falls to teachers who are not members of the regular faculty . . . Average class size has been increasing. There seems to be a "point of no return" after which research, consulting, graduate instruction became so absorbing that faculty efforts can no longer be concentrated in undergraduate instruction as they once were. This process has been going on for a long time; federal research funds have intensified it. As a consequence, undergraduate education is more likely to be acceptable than outstanding; educational policy from the undergraduate point of view is largely neglected. How to escape the cruel paradox that a superior faculty results in an inferior concern for undergraduate teaching is one of our more pressing problems.[7]

Kerr saw this as a "pressing problem." In fact, it is much more like a major catastrophe, a state of affairs with troubling implications for students and society alike. For all his candor in identifying some of the educational defects of the modern university, Kerr only scratched the surface. A closer examination of education in the multiversity reveals a far grimmer reality than than portrayed in *The Uses of the University*. What follows in the present book is an account of this educational reality and an inquiry into some of its primary underlying causes.

It is important to note that shortly after the publication of Kerr's book, the Berkeley campus exploded in one of the most dramatic examples of student rebellion in American history. Beyond the initial free speech issues, thousands of students focused on the educational inadequacies of the University of California. The Free Speech Movement was the major catalyst for a more general national consideration of educational defects in American universities. In the ensuing decade after the 1964 outbreak at Berkeley, there were hundreds of student demonstrations throughout the country about a wide range of political, social, and educational issues. Racism and the war in Viet Nam, of course, were central to these conflicts. Still, the focal point of many student protests was the movement for educational change and reform. The post-FSM era saw countless proposals for improving education, including more recognition for teaching, student representation on educational policy committees, and interdisciplinary alternatives to academic orthodoxy at large, prestigious research universities. The era also generated hundreds of official commissions, investigations, and committees as well as a massive barrage of public rhetoric about the need to promote better undergraduate education.

Some of this activity was instrumental in effecting serious improvement. The record in major research institutions, however, has been far more modest. Undergraduate education has deteriorated in the two decades since Kerr identified it as a troublesome problem. In many schools, the educational defects identified during the 1960's remain; many, indeed, have been exacerbated during the past decade. All too often, the heralded "improvements" have involved little more than the establishment of a few token programs, projects, and cumbersome bureaucratic entities purportedly designed for instructional development. Many are created more to provide public relations gloss than to address serious and complex educational problems. In many universities since the 60's and 70's, innovative programs have been created, permitted to endure for a few years, then phased out and replaced by new programs. Meanwhile, little of permanent value remains and the underlying structural causes are rarely addressed.

Mediocrity characterizes the state of education at most large American research universities today. These institutions are renowned almost exclusively for the publications of their faculty members and their stature as scholars in their various academic fields. As Kerr and other defenders of contemporary academic life indicate, this is clearly advantageous in several ways. What they overlook, however, is that this orientation has made undergraduate education a matter of enormous institutional neglect.

Most undergraduates can ruefully attest to the major difficulties: disorganized, uninspiring, and boring teaching, sloppy or non-existent advising, and a general disregard for the academic and other pursuits of undergraduate students. This has come to pass in part because there is a pervasive indifference to students and a lack of genuine concern about

11

teaching in the modern university. In my own work at the University of California, I have seen literally thousands of students victimized by these attitudes. Scarcely a week goes by without several students confiding to me about their own educational disappointments and the personal frustrations that inevitably accompany them.

Regularly, students (often the best and brightest of them) tell me how they must endure classes in which professors merely repeat information already assigned in course readings; how they are made to feel unwelcome during office hours; how they are treated in class and elsewhere with ridicule, derision, or patronizing amusement; how their questions remain unanswered; and how, through various verbal and non-verbal forms of communication, they are viewed as irritants who impede the "real" work of academic life. My desire is not to be overly dramatic here. The sad reality, however, is that I have heard countless such complaints from students over the years. They have come from young men and women who have no reason to distort or in any way compromise the truth of their allegations.

The hostility to teaching and to students is more insidiously manifested in the daily comments of many university faculty members and administrators. Once again, in the interest of fairness, I must note that this is not a universal phenomenon. There are many professors who enjoy teaching and who like their contact with undergraduates. Still, these distressing attitudes are endemic to the institution. In universities, as in all organizations, real values emerge most strikingly in private social settings. Professors and administrators often disclose their most honest feelings in office corridors, dinner parties, luncheon gatherings, sporting and cultural events, and similar contexts. I have been privy to hundreds of such circumstances and have regularly heard my academic colleagues discuss their personal attitudes about various features of their work. More often than not, I have found their remarks about teaching undergraduates frightening in their implications.

At Berkeley, for example, I listened to many faculty members express their irritation at having to teach at all. I watched many of them scheme to avoid literally any undergraduate obligations. In these informal settings, I regularly noticed that personal status would rise in direct proportion to the extent that such avoidance was successful.

Without exaggeration, it is fair to conclude that hundreds of Berkeley professors would be delighted to be relieved of their obligation to teach undergraduates. In a memorable meeting with students in the late 70's, a Berkeley Dean said to them that if they really wanted good teaching, they should leave and enroll in one of the local junior colleges. This cavalier attitude, unfortunately, only mirrored the private remarks of many of his colleagues.

The values at UCLA appear disturbingly similar. Regularly, my faculty colleagues complain about bothersome undergraduates. On several occasions, I have been told by professors that they prefer the campus during the summer, when most students are traditionally away on vacation. With considerable skill, like their Berkeley counterparts, they pawn their students off to inexperienced teaching assistants and to student service personnel, whose ranks have grown in response to the unwillingness of professors to participate in undergraduate affairs. From my own visits and conversations, I believe that this same dubious process obtains at comparable multiversities throughout the country.

These faculty attitudes reflect and reinforce the fundamental lack of thinking about education in the modern research university. It is ironic that an institution purportedly dedicated to education and intellectual enlightenment spends so little time considering the meaning of education. In my seventeen years of teaching at the University of California, I have had serious, sustained educational conversations with no more than ten or twelve colleagues. While I have, of course, fleetingly discussed educational matters with many others, they have almost always been on superficial topics that do not address basic questions and values. Typically, they are confined to specific, nuts-and-bolts problems: how many students should be in a particular class; how many books are appropriate in a ten-week quarter; what are the merits of essay questions and multiple-choice examinations; what mechanisms can best prevent plagiarism and other forms of cheating; and many other questions that, while important, are hardly profound. The reason that so little attention is given to more serious educational problems is simply that they are not considered important. This is inevitable in universities where education is a mere adjunct to other intellectual activities.

As Clark Kerr has indicated, other than educational values have come to dominate the modern university. The present infatuation with rankings and prestige, exemplified by the response of the UCLA community to its number five designation from the Associated Research Council, is ubiquitous. At academic conferences and conventions, professors from "leading" universities talk incessantly about ratings, not unlike football coaches striving to crack the weekly top ten. Numerous conversations are held about attracting big name scholars to specific universities in the hope that ratings will rise. "Visibility," more than anything else, has become the paramount objective of individual professors and individual universities alike.

An entrepeneurial spirit pervades the affairs of the modern university, a spirit that is intimately connected to the lust for status and institutional prestige. It is manifested in the competition to obtain research money and to generate spheres of scholarly influence and domination. What it means operationally is that large numbers of university professors have in essence become businesspersons rather than educators. In their quest for grant support from government agencies and private foundations, they have adopted the behaviors and increasingly the attitudes of the commercial world. Significant amounts of time, for example, are spent in the search for funds, necessitating the hiring of grant experts and subordinate academic personnel to do the actual research work and much of the daily instruction. In pursuit of academic recognition, faculty members have become almost indistinguishable from public relations experts. Professors now shamelessly promote themselves much in the way that advertising executives market commodities. Success along these lines elevates personal and institutional standing and contributes to the low priority of local educational concerns.

A business mentality may well be useful in a variety of social settings in the modern world. In general, however, it is inimical to the process of education. It deflects attention from the intellectual needs of students, fosters savage competition that inhibits educational collaboration, and focuses personal energies in largely inappropriate directions. Sadly, however, strong institutional incentives ensure that entrepeneurship will continue to command the allegiance of academic men and women seeking visibility and professional status.

Another feature of this business mentality has more subtle anti-educational implications. University professors are as attracted to fads and fashions as any other group of human beings. At any given time, there are acceptable lines of research and investigation. Certain intellectual approaches and theories are in vogue, while others have passed their days of glory or have yet to emerge to the level of popular acceptance. Prestige and grants tend to inure to those professors capable of conforming to whatever is dominant at the time. Like effective salespersons everywhere, many academics will tailor their products to the requirements of the marketplace. In far too many cases, faculty members respond to requests for proposals regardless of whether they have any intrinsic interest in the subject matter of the proposals. The effect of all this is to promote an ambience of orthodoxy in academic affairs.[8] It is important to note that any orthodoxy defeats the aims of education. When certain lines of intellectual work are encouraged by marketplace forces and others are disparaged or unrewarded, a stultifying environment prevails. It is a negation of the state of free inquiry that should properly characterize the academic enterprise. Inevitably, the entrepeneurial perspectives of the faculty will color the entire range of educational offerings to undergraduate students.

These attitudes and practices thus encourage the post-war research university to become instruments of mass, alienated training. In many respects, the results are the antithesis of serious education. At major research universities, thousands of undergraduates shuffle from one large lecture class to another, often tragically unaware of the existence of imaginative alternatives to such educational passivity. What has disturbed me most over the years is that many of these students cannot even conceive that their educations could be infinitely superior. They are the prisoners in the updated version of Plato's *Allegory of the Cave*.

In multiversity classes, undergraduates are often taught by faculty members unconcerned about the process of learning and eager to resume their personal research. These courses place a premium on note-taking and memorization, often on information likely to be obsolete a few years later. Students are thus encouraged to be little more than passive educational consumers, with little incentive to engage in critical analysis or independent investigation. They are trained to accept what is

15

given and to minimize confrontations with the established order in all academic fields.

Over a period of four or more years, certain habits of mind and patterns of behavior develop as a result of such educational passivity. What these students learn above all is a subtle process of adaptation. Young men and women who uncritically accept the role of disengaged consumers will easily conform to whatever values are provided to them by the dominant institutions of social, economic, and political life. Passivity begets more passivity, and students molded by their inadequate experiences in higher "learning" easily become uncritical citizens in general. Their academic degrees signify a mere ability to persist in an organizational environment for a substantial period of time. In a world beset with awesome and complex problems, society needs people capable of something more than memorizing information and adjusting to bureaucratic requirements. More than ever before, society demands men and women who are unafraid of taking risks and of questioning established policies. The present priorities of America's research universities make it unlikely that such people will emerge in large numbers from those institutions.

The wide public assumption that the sharp educational criticism of the 1960's wrought major reforms in university education is understandable but inaccurate. It is therefore a matter of urgency to correct this misimpression by examining the structure of academic life even more thoroughly. Such an inquiry into the underlying reasons for the failures of higher education has profound implications for society generally. The following chapters will show how some structural elements of the modern university are responsible for these dangerous failures. A closer view of the present organizational system and of the character and personalities of academic personnel will demonstrate, in particular, why the university has moved so far from its mandate to educate its students - the people who come, innocently and eagerly, for a purpose that has long since faded into obscurity and irrelevance.

NOTES

1. There are many excellent sources that explain the methods and spirit of qualitative social science. See, for example, Leonard Schatzman and Anselm Strauss, *Field Research: Strategies for a Natural Sociology*, 1973; George McCall and J. L. Simmons, editors, *Issues in Participant Observation: A Text and Reader*, 1969; John Lofland, *Analyzing Social Settings: A Guide to Qualitative Observation and Analysis* , 1971; Monica B. Morris, *An Excursion into Creative Sociology*, 1977; and Jack D. Douglas, *Investigative Social Research: Individual and Team Research*, 1976.

2. There is a vast and impressive body of literature in this critical tradition. Some important examples include Robert Lynd, *Knowledge For What?*, 1939; C. Wright Mills,*White Collar*, 1951; C. Wright Mills, *The Power Elite*, 1956; Gabriel Kolko, *Wealth and Power in America*, 1962; Herbert Marcuse, *One-Dimensional Man*, 1964; Herbert Schiller, *Mass Communications and American Empire*, 1969; Herbert Schiller, *The Mind Managers,* 1973; Barbara Ehrenreich and Deirdre English, *For Her Own Good*, 1978; and numerous others. Books and essays by Christopher Lasch, Barry Commoner, William A. Williams, Louis Kampf, Stephen Jay Gould, and H. Bruce Franklin have also contributed significantly to this tradition. Various outstanding journalists such as I. F. Stone, Vance Packard, Fred J. Cook, Jessica Mitford, Nicholas Von Hoffman, Robert Scheer, and others also add stature to critical social inquiry. Their efforts, sometimes ignored or patronized in academic circles, deserve wide attention.

3. Some significant examples of this strain of work centering on the defects of academic disciplines include C. Wright Mills, *The Sociological Imagination*, 1959; J. David Colfax and Jack L. Roach, editors, *Radical Sociology*, 1971; Alfred McClung Lee, *Sociology For Whom?*, 1978; Theodore Roszak, editor, *The Dissenting Academy*, 1967; and Louis Kampf and Paul Lauter, editors, *The Politics of Literature*, 1970. Internal critiques of the legal profession include Fred Rodell, *Woe*

17

Unto You, Lawyers, 1939; Robert Lefcourt, editor, *Law Against The People*, 1971; and Jonathan Black, editor, *Radical Lawyers*, 1971. Medical examples include Thomas Preston, *The Clay Pedestal*, 1981 and Robert S. Mendelsohn, *Male Practice*, 1981. There are numerous books and articles critical of other professions and institutions.

4. Once again, the literature of this tradition is immense. The following are a small sample of critical analyses of various aspects of university values, policies, and operations: Thorstein Veblen, *The Higher Learning in America,* 1918; Upton Sinclair, *The Goose Step: A Study of American Education*, 1922; Jose Ortega y Gasset, *Mission of the University*, 1930; Robert Hutchins, *The Higher Learning in America*, 1936; Robert Hutchins, *The University of Utopia,* 1953; Paul Goodman, *The Community of Scholars,* 1962; Nicholas Von Hoffman, *The Multiversity,* 1966; Robert Paul Wolff, *The Ideal of the University* , 1969; Sheldon Wolin and John Schaar, *The Berkeley Rebellion and Beyond,* 1970; Joseph Fashing and Steven Deutsch, *Academics in Retreat,* 1971; Bettina Aptheker, *The Academic Rebellion in the United States*, 1972; Ira Shor, *Critical Teaching and Everyday Life,* 1980. This list merely scratches the surface, and there is a much greater body of periodical literature along these lines.

5. Clark Kerr, *The Uses of the University* (Cambridge, Massachusetts: Harvard University Press, 1963), pp.118-119.

6. Ibid., p.114.

7. Ibid., p.65.

8. See Chapter 4 for an expanded treatment of academic othodoxy, especially in the realm of faculty retention and promotion policies.

CHAPTER 2

University Organization and Educational Neglect

For many centuries, philosophers and educators have written and debated about ideal forms of education. They have proposed, with varying results, an extraordinary variety of organizational schemes to accomplish their goals of higher learning. From Plato in *The Republic* to Cardinal Newman in *The Idea of the University* to Robert Hutchins' experiments at the University of Chicago, theorists and academic leaders have sought ways to promote the liberal arts tradition of Western civilization. In the past, most of these efforts have been in the service of a particular vision of education - an idea that would be the soul of the academic enterprise.

According to Clark Kerr, the days of vision are long gone. The time when a university could have a single animating principle is, to Dr. Kerr, a vestige of a bygone era, a romantic notion incompatible with the realities of the twentieth century. For him, the modern university is intrinsically a pluralist and specialized enterprise serving a wide variety of communities and interests. As a predominantly research entity, it must orient its operations, and thus its organizational structure, to the needs of its various constituencies.

There is no question that the contemporary research university is involved in activities far beyond the imagination of the educators of the past. Kerr's description twenty years ago of the University of California reveals some of the major changes in institutional concerns and operations:

> The University of California last year had operating expenditures from all sources of nearly half a billion dollars, with almost another 100 million for construction; a total employment of over 40,000 people, more than IBM and in a far greater variety of

endeavors; operations in over a hundred locations, counting campuses, experiment stations, agricultural and urban extension services, and projects involving more than fifty countries; nearly 10,000 courses in its catalogues; some form of contact with nearly every industry, nearly every level of government, nearly every person in its region. Vast amounts of expensive equipment were serviced and maintained. Over 4000 babies were born in its hospitals. It is the world's largest purveyor of white mice. It will soon have the world's largest primate colony. It will soon also have 100,000 students - 30,000 of them at the graduate level; yet much less than one third of its expenditures are directly related to teaching. It already has nearly 200,000 students in extension courses - including one out of every three lawyers and one out of every six doctors in the state.[1]

Two decades later, of course, the figures are much greater and the level of activities even more extensive. Like other multiversities, the University of California is a complex corporate unit that needs an organizational structure to deal with its multifaceted functions. This structure is designed to accomplish diverse, highly specific goals as efficiently as possible. Under these circumstances, organization on behalf of a unifying educational vision is simply out of the question. The reason is obvious: education is merely one feature of a university devoted to a far broader range of intellectual, social, and economic activities.

A closer view of the organization of this complex institution is useful in demonstrating why undergraduate education can only be a marginal concern at best. The very pattern of university organization ensures that students will not receive the kind of broad and integrated education demanded at the threshold of the twenty first century. Universities are typically organized along extremely specialized lines in order to cater to the many interest groups vying for resources and status. This leads inexorably to a highly bureaucratized structure more responsive to political pressure and less hospitable to educational leadership.

Two specific features of the organization of the multiversity are particularly significant in fostering educational mediocrity.

The first is the character of academic organization, specifically the departmental domination of university life. The second is the enormous administrative apparatus of the research university. Together, these structural elements have combined to determine priorities, condition attitudes, and even alter human behavior and personality. As I shall show, the implications for undergraduate students are depressing.

By tradition, academic institutions are organized by departments dealing with specialized areas of human knowledge. Even a casual glance through a college or university catalogue reveals how this system works. In a small college, there are typically such standard academic departments as English, history, philosophy, psychology, political science, economics, biology, chemistry, mathematics, physics and several others. In large research universities, this departmental arrangement is more complex and highly specialized.

In the humanities area, for example, there are usually departments of English, German, French, Oriental languages, Spanish, Slavic, philosophy, music, art history, and others. In the social science area, it is usual to find departments of political science, sociology, psychology, anthropology, linguistics, geography, and many more. The natural sciences particularly lend themselves to specialization of function. Typical are departments of biochemistry, physiology, botany, zoology, entomology, microbiology, statistics, geology, geophysics, and even additional scientific disciplines.

Multiversities, furthermore, generally have professional schools such as public health, social welfare, nursing, engineering, city planning, librarianship, law, medicine, education, and others. These too are sometimes organized along departmental lines. For example, engineering schools often contain departments of electrical engineering, nuclear and thermal engineering, computer science, materials science, and mechanics and structures. Each of these departments, both in arts and sciences and in professional schools, is a budgetary unit with its own parochial interests and intellectual territory. Each, moreover, must compete with the rest for general institutional resources.

Because knowledge is so immense today, this departmental system would seem to be a rational arrangement for the organization of academic affairs. Since no human being can deal effectively with more than a relatively small part of knowledge, it is obvious that some specialized mechanism must be available for the creation and dissemination of knowledge. Academic disciplines oriented to specific subjects and topics perform these roles in all American research universities.

Over the years, this departmental structure has come to dominate the university's academic affairs. There is no question that departmental hegemony has had many advantages. It has promoted rigorous, specialized knowledge in an astonishing array of fields. It has enabled academic men and women to develop a genuine sense of professional identity. It would be unfair to suggest, therefore, that the departmental organization is an unmitigated evil, a perspective sometimes fostered by academics preferring interdisciplinary modes of thought and academic organization.

At the same time, there are severe limitations to this present departmental arrangement. Students and the general public are ordinarily unaware that the division of intellectual functions into academic departments is an arbitrary process that often defeats broader educational goals. Many academic disciplines are the result of historical accidents. Many were the creations of strong academic personalities seeking their own territory as a catalyst for selfish career mobility.[2] There is nothing intrinsically compelling about English or economics or biology as the sole focus of intellectual inquiry. Such fields in fact are little more than a convenient form of administrative organization, one of a variety of possibile ways to structure academic affairs.

The present system tends to work to the disadvantage of most university undergraduates. This culture of extreme specialization provides a fragmented curriculum that distorts perceptions about the actual complexities of human existence. Life itself rarely breaks down neatly into those expedient but artificial categories called academic departments.[3] Indeed, many modern problems far transcend these divisions. The crisis in energy, for example, cuts across such fields as physics, geology, economics, political science, anthropology, psychology, and several others. Specialized knowledge from any one of these disciplines, while useful in a more comprehensive resolution of this problem, is severely incapable of addressing the problem by itself. Similarly, the issue of nuclear war cuts across such fields as political science, psychology, radiology, history, and others. In a recent UCLA seminar on this topic, authorities from the fields of medicine, politics, psychiatry, and the humanities sought to help students examine this phenomenon in an integrated way. A perspective from merely one academic discipline would clearly have been inadequate.

University officials, however, perceive accomplishments in specific academic fields as the highest form of intellectual endeavor. Rewards are provided for specialized work within these disciplines. Inevitably, the attitudes and values that emerge from this structure color the entire educational process. With only rare exceptions, faculty members believe that their sole obligation is merely to teach their particular disciplines. Their view is that students must develop their own framework to integrate materials and theories from the various fields. This attitude, however, is unrealistic. If most professors, trained as they are to be specialists in specific disciplines, are not themselves integrated learners, there is no reason to expect their less qualified students to be. Indeed, it is professionally irresponsible to assume that undergraduates will assimilate knowledge from a wide variety of fields coherently without specific encouragement and concrete faculty assistance. Many contemporary professors agree with this observation; few take any steps to implement appropriate change in this direction.

These faculty attitudes and practices, generated by the departmental organization of the modern university, have other dubious educational implications. Far too many professors teach as if all their students are to become future Ph.D.'s in their specific academic disciplines. The overwhelming majority of undergraduates, however, even at the most prestigious schools, are unlikely to become scholars and professors. Instead, they aspire to become doctors, lawyers, business executives, civil servants, engineers, journalists, and the like. Teaching discrete academic disciplines alone, in the absence of a broader educational perspective, misses the point. These thousands of undergraduate students, above all, need a sound general education devoted to critical analysis and effective written and oral communication. An exposure to front line research in specific fields is undeniably useful. Even more important, however, is a coherent sense of the

23

relationships of the social sciences, the humanities, the natural sciences, and the arts, all within a broad historical and ethical framework. To accomplish this objective requires enormous institutional and individual effort. The narrow departmental focus of the multiversity militates in the opposite direction. The poorly educated men and women emerging from the present system are likely to be increasingly frustrated by the challenges of a complex technological society.

The extreme fragmentation of knowledge, furthermore, impedes any general faculty concern about broader educational problems. When professors are preoccupied almost exclusively with their sub-fields in chemistry, art history, or anthropology, there is no incentive or even time to worry about connections with other fields. The result is that professors rarely even think about the need for a broadly integrated education, much less the means by which this goal could be implemented. Ironically, the more accomplished many scholars become in their own fields, the more ineffective they become as educators.

Departmental domination also encourages extreme territoriality among university faculty members, a phenomenon that only exacerbates the pattern of defective education. Professors are often careful to draw tight lines around their specific areas of academic expertise. Highly protective, they are distrustful of those who would cross the borders from one discipline to another. At UCLA, for example, I have heard ethicists in the philosophy department express irritation and nervousness that medical school faculty members would deal with medical ethics - an area, presumably, reserved exclusively for certified philosophy professors. Virtually any interdisciplinary effort encounters similar resistance from scholars guarding their own turf. These attitudes are hardly conducive to the kind of academic cooperation that would better serve university undergraduates.

Territoriality frequently leads to hostility towards the intellectual labors of colleagues in other fields. This phenomenon pervades the modern research university, further widening the gap between educational potential and educational reality. Examples of such hostility are legion. It is common to hear physicists, geologists, and mathematicians talk disparagingly of the work of professors of French and sociology. A frequent refrain is that literary scholars and

24

social scientists are unable to produce solid evidence for their propositions and conclusions. It is equally common to hear art historians and philosophers speak scorningly of the efforts of chemists and botanists. They regularly complain that these natural scientists are indifferent to and contemptuous of cultural and aesthetic achievements. This academic sniping exists even within broadly related areas of human knowledge. Historians constantly complain about the narrowness of political scientists and sociologists regularly express their disdain for psychologists - and vice versa. And this phenomenon even occurs within specific academic disciplines. Scholars, for example, in such sub-fields as political behavior feel intellectually superior to their colleagues in political theory - and, again, vice versa.

It is common for people in any field to defend their activities and reject those of others. In the modern university, this phenomenon is ubiquitous to the point of educational tragedy. If these attitudes were kept relatively quiet, they would be harmless. The rigid departmental organization of the university, however, seems to intensify such parochial identities and values. Hostility to other academic fields is regularly conveyed to students in classrooms and offices, thus generating a widespread ambience of intolerance. When this is internalized (as it often is) by students themselves, it reduces intellectual curiosity and eliminates the motivation to build bridges between different scholarly methods and traditions. An excessive concern, moreover, with the defects of others' academic specialties makes it even more unlikely that professors will cooperate in broader, more integrated educational endeavors.

The primacy of departments defeats education in still other ways. Kerr was correct in noting that faculty members in the contemporary university "are less members of the particular university and more colleagues within their national discipline groups."[4] This seemingly innocuous reality, which has intensified since Dr. Kerr delivered his lectures at Harvard in 1963, has awesome consequences for the educations of millions of American undergraduates.

It is important to explore this byproduct of the departmental domination of university organization in depth. When a professor identifies more as a member of an academic field than as a member of a local educational community, certain attitudes and actions inevitably follow. In research institutions, the advancement of knowledge in particular disciplines is the overriding focus of a faculty member's career. Professors of history, for example, perceive of themselves as historians far more than as teachers of history. This subtle difference often means that "lesser" activities, such as undergraduate education, will provide minimal gratification and little if any recognition beyond the campus community.

Therein lies a key problem. Recognition and visibility have been established as the primary focus of academic careers in the circuit of prestigious American universities. Almost without exception, such recognition results from research publication in specific fields. A professor of psychology or linguistics at UCLA is thus much more concerned about how he or she is perceived by psychologists or linguists at Harvard, Yale, Columbia, and Berkeley than by students at UCLA. The former determines one's academic standing throughout the world. The latter, at best, affects one's personal feelings about teaching. It has no bearing whatever on professional recognition in the field.

Academic organization oriented to specific disciplinary concerns ensures that external sources of professional validation will prevail. All fields have a hierarchy of journals that confer appropriate status on the authors of research reports appearing within them. Professors are understandably eager to have their work accepted in the most prestigious publications, for it will evoke national or even international attention. Similarly important are favorable reviews of books and monographs by known authorities in the same field. References to one's own work in the research publications of others also promote higher professional visibility.

Regional and national conferences of academic specialists represent another external source of standing in the competitive world of research scholarship. Presentations of papers at these affairs can be extremely helpful in career advancement. To be well received by peers at the Modern Language Association, the American Physical Society, or the American Political Science Association can have profound professional implications. Word spreads quickly among faculty members in specific academic disciplines throughout the country. This is why immense amounts of time and energy are spent on the preparation of papers for these scholarly conventions.

Grantsmanship has also come to play a crucial role in academic visibility. One's capacity to attract money for research from major governmental agencies and private foundations enhances prestige, especially in times of fiscal constraint in higher education. Once again, substantial faculty efforts are expended in this direction. At any given moment, thousands of university professors are preparing complex grant proposals in their quest to obtain or reinforce their recognition within their fields. They know well that a sound track record in this domain will have a ripple effect in all aspects of their careers as research scholars.

Publications, conventions, and grants all represent external forms of professional activity and identification. This system has become so dominant today that many professors are utterly indifferent to the daily affairs and problems of their home campuses. Their consummate concerns about developments in their personal disciplines make it difficult for them to worry about purely local educational issues. Indeed, for thousands of American faculty members, their local campus is a mere base of operations providing salary and incidental support for their global academic enterprises.

The outward focus of university professors has inevitable and negative implications for undergraduate education. Over the years, internal activity directed towards educational goals has been fundamentally devalued. To be blunt, efforts on campus that are not directly tied to the established sources of external validation are useless in career terms. Teaching, for example, no matter how excellent it may be, can only generate a local reputation. One's effectiveness with undergraduate students becomes rapidly known in that community, but it rarely transcends that level of recognition. A professor at the University of Chicago or the Massachusetts Institute of Technology who is asked to evaluate the work of a disciplinary colleague at UCLA probably knows little and cares even less about his or her teaching record. In fact, a letter of praise from an authority at Harvard or Yale is probably worth more than five years of outstanding teaching evaluations. The present scheme of academic organization in the multiversity thus ensures the marginality of educational priorities.

27

There is also a darker side of this arrangement. A widespread attitude exists among academics that almost anyone can teach, but only first-rate professors can achieve national and international reputations. The effects of this view are both obvious and dangerous. In the culture of the modern research university, daily classroom and related obligations are treated as pedestrian concerns, to be handled by anyone of journeyman academic standing. Hundreds of thousands of university undergraduates, unfortunately, pay a lifelong price for their professors' collective shortsightedness.

Not only is teaching itself devalued because it is merely local, but virtually anything confined to a single university campus remains subordinate in the hierarchy of academic values. There is thus little incentive for career purposes to participate in systematic efforts to improve instruction at one's home campus. Nor is there much incentive to even think about the problems of undergraduate education or discuss these matters with faculty colleagues. The triumph of external professional validation has taken its toll. Thousands of American university professors simply ignore local educational problems because there is no percentage in it for them. It is well to recognize that professors are no different from other upwardly mobile professionals. They usually do what is rewarded and usually refrain from doing what is not.

There is yet another regrettable byproduct of the departmental organization of the multiversity. Graduate level instruction, tied directly to the research function of the institution, is clearly the top educational priority at places like Berkeley and UCLA. Graduate students have a higher status than undergraduate students and their academic and personal needs are generally given more careful attention by university officials.

The award of teaching assistantships is a traditional way for research universities to support graduate students working for doctoral degrees in specific fields. This serves a double purpose in most university settings. First, it provides financial assistance to the students selected to become teaching assistants. Second, it relieves some serious instructional pressures. Many courses in large universities have hundreds of students. Mass and impersonal, these classes are characterized by the educational passivity described in Chapter 1. There is therefore a desperate need to employ inexpensive academic personnel to teach smaller discussion sections and to grade examinations and papers. In the past twenty years, teaching assistants have played an increasingly important role in the educational lives of university undergraduates.

In theory, the use of teaching assistants makes enormous sense. Given the existence of large lecture classes, it is useful to have smaller sections where undergraduates can interact with more mature academic men and women. It is also desirable for graduate students to serve an apprenticeship as undergraduate teachers. Those who continue in academic careers will likely benefit from this experience and may become more effective teachers when they hold regular faculty positions.

Theory and practice often diverge, however. The selection of teaching assistants is rarely a function of demonstrated interest or competence in undergraduate education. On the contrary, it is typically viewed by academic departments as convenient employment for graduate students continuing the "real" business of graduate work - research and the more subtle process of socialization into the values of specific academic disciplines.

These circumstances produce entirely fortuitous educational results. Graduate students employed as teaching assistants are often under intense pressures that ensure that serious conflicts will arise. Even though undergraduate teaching is the paramount responsibility of their positions, these graduate students must also finish their own doctoral work in order to compete for regular academic positions. The entire range of teaching commitment and personal responsibility exists among teaching assistants in large research universities. Some are exceptional teachers, who combine personal vigor and intellectual excitement for lower division students. They take their role seriously and are often far superior to the regular professors for whom they work. Others, however, are preoccupied with their own research and tend to slight or even ignore their teaching and advising obligations. At many universities, some do not even have a proper command of the English language, rendering their teaching work largely useless. Scores of complaints from my UCLA students have convinced me that this problem is not trivial, especially in mathematics and the natural sciences. The haphazard educational effectiveness of these apprentice undergraduate

29

teachers reflects the lack of institutional commitment to education generally. Any other result is impossible in light of the division of academic life into arbitrary disciplinary fiefdoms.

This departmental domination of the university is not the sole organizational foundation for educational indifference and mediocrity. Since the end of World War II (but especially since the Soviet Union launched Sputnik), the overall structure of the university has changed dramatically. There has been a phenomenal growth of non-academic departments, divisions, institutes, and other administrative units within the multiversity. The result is a truly monumental bureaucratic apparatus that has had a profound effect upon the daily educational operations of the institution.

It is instructive to examine this modern phenomenon in some detail. A careful look into just how extensive university bureaucracy has become helps to explain why education can rarely be a serious priority. The massive proliferation of non-academic entities has fundamentally altered university existence. It has spawned a new administrative work force whose impact on academic affairs has been equally profound. This modern phenomenon is only vaguely understood by undergraduate students and even less by the general public. The remainder of this chapter, therefore, will analyze the unfortunate consequences of bureaucratized higher education.

All major research universities fall within this category. The example of UCLA, therefore, is far from unique. Its large, cumbersome, and basically unmanageable bureaucracy is all too indicative of the present state of American higher learning. A brief perusal of the administrative organization chart provides a glimpse into the 1980's version of Kerr's multiversity. At the central level at UCLA, there is a Chancellor's Office, with a substantial budget and support staff. There is also an Executive Vice Chancellor, to whom an enormous number of subordinates report. There are, for example, Vice Chancellors or Assistant Vice Chancellors for Institutional Relations, Planning, Business, Community Safety, Finance, Research, Instructional Development, Student Affairs, Faculty Relations, Staff Personnel, Graduate Programs, Public Affairs, and several others. Each of these administrative officials in turn has a substantial support staff and numerous subordinates. Such operations generally have large budgets, since salaries at these managerial levels are comparatively high.

A few more specific examples illustrate the complexity of the bureaucratic apparatus of the modern university. At UCLA, for instance, there is an Assistant Vice Chancellor for Business. Under his or her direction are such offices as the Administrative Services Manager; the Housing and Food Services Director; the Vending Services Manager; the Central Word Processing Manager; Insurance and Risk Management Coordinator; the Mail and Messenger Service Manager; the Telecommunications Manager; the Contracts and Grants Administration Director; the Materiel Director; the Transportation Service Administrator; and the Parking Services Manager.

The Assistant Vice Chancellor for Finance commands a comparable bureaucratic empire. Reporting to that senior-level official are the Accounting Officer; the Central Collections Representative; the Disbursements Manager; Payroll and Employee Benefits Manager; Student Services Accounting Manager; the Financial Review Officer, the Main Cashier and Operational Assistance Officer; and several other administrators. Each of these offices, once again, controls substantial budgets and has large numbers of staff employees.

In recent years, the general area of student services has grown monumentally. UCLA is again typical. At the top of this particular bureaucratic hierarchy is a Vice Chancellor for Student Affairs, who oversees a multi-million dollar operation with many subordinate units and hundreds of employees. The following units fall within the ambit of this office: Undergraduate Admissions and Relations with Schools; Financial Aid Director; Director of Placement and Career Planning; Dean of Residential Life; Director of Student Loan Services and Collections; Assistant Vice Chancellor for Student Development; Registrar[5]; Psychological and Counseling Service; Dean of Students; Director of Extramural Programs and Opportunities Center; Director of Organizational and Inter-organizational Relations; Director of Program Review, Education, and Research; Student Health Services; Student Advocacy and Assistance (Women's Resource Center, Student Legal Services, etc.); and, once more, several other administrative units.

This only scratches the surface. There are large bureaucratic structures for the library, for intercollegiate athletics (especially at UCLA, where this enterprise has historically been a matter of extremely high priority), for development and fund raising, and for other functions. In addition, the major units in the academic programs are highly bureaucratized. The College of Letters and Science and all eleven of UCLA's professional schools have large administrative components. The Schools of Engineering and Medicine, for example, have more administrators with more bureaucratic units and support staff than many smaller American colleges and universities.

In fairness, it must be noted that there are many external reasons for this spectacular growth of bureaucracy in the modern research university. These offices did not emerge as a result of a deliberate conspiracy to create vast superstructures and empires. In some ways, the growth of academic bureaucracy is a function of life in the late twentieth century, an inevitable feature of advanced industrial society. Furthermore, many administrative offices in the university have been established in response to federal and state laws, regulations, and policies. Contract and grant offices are good examples. In order to compete effectively for funds offered by government agencies and private foundations, it is essential to have a central coordinating office on campus to provide information, assist in preparation, and ensure compliance with financial and other requirements. Indeed, many internal university operations are mandated by law. Affirmative action offices, for example, were created in order to deal with legitimate federal, state, and local regulations designed to address racial and sexual discrimination, problems as common to higher education as to any other American institutions. Finally, many student service units grew in response to the educational and political agitation of the 1960's and 1970's. Thus in accommodating the multifaceted demands of society since the end of World War II, the university has increasingly assumed corporate forms in responding to various external and internal constituencies.

Regardless of the reasons, however, the colossal increase in the administrative organization of the university has had a powerfully negative impact on education. Above all, the sheer size of academic bureaucracy, perhaps necessary to run the multiversity (or comparable large organization), has impeded quality instruction and has served as a major barrier to the educational needs of undergraduate students. All large organizations tend to spawn units that become ends in themselves, subtly transforming and eventually defeating the articulated objectives of the institution as a whole. Instead, large bureaucracies begin to exist for themselves alone. Rather than functioning to advance broader aims, they become devoted to their own preservation and growth. There is nothing deliberately malicious in this process, for it is a natural phenomenon of bureaucracy. In that respect, universities are no different from other organizations. Just as the personnel in various Motor Vehicle Departments sometimes forget that they have a human constituency, so too do academic bureaucrats regularly forget that they are dealing with the legitimate educational needs of real human beings.[6]

Size generates many other consequences that adversely affect education and learning. All bureaucracies foster territorial claims, immense paperwork, personality conflicts, and petty political intrigues. These results occur in General Motors, in the United States Department of Health and Human Services, in the Los Angeles County Department of Welfare, in the District of Columbia Department of Transportation, in Her Majesty's Immigration Service in Great Britain, in the Bibliotheque Nationale in Paris, in the Financial Aid Offices at the University of California at Berkeley and Los Angeles, and so on throughout the world. These realities assume a life of their own, far beyond the ostensible requirements of specific jobs and the responsibilities of administrative units.

When administrators spend time, as they invariably do, protecting their own turf, they have less time to devote to what they are supposed in principle to be doing. There is a ubiquitous process of seeking more money and staff resources (or minimizing cutbacks in times of fiscal stress) and to create personal bureaucratic empires. The quest for power leads administrators to fight off encroachments and competition from other internal units within the large organizational scheme. In the multiversity, these activities reduce the institutional and personal commitment to broader educational objectives.

The same thing occurs in the area of personality struggles and office politics. Virtually anyone who has worked in organizations knows well the emotional and other consequences of these phenomena. Internal power conflicts cause employees to form long and short term alliances to preserve their positions or obtain promotions with higher pay and status. Inevitably, people come to revile and despise others, scheming to deny them advancement or even their very employment. At any moment in any university, there are hundreds of these corrosive affairs. Who is out to get whom occupies a tremendous amount of time in academic settings. Not only do these intrigues deflect attention from educational operations, but they also create a psychological environment throughout the institution that can only inhibit a concern for human learning.

Sheer size also fosters immense waste, inefficiency, and mismanagement. Scale alone makes it difficult for the multiversity to address educational needs systematically and effectively. Insiders in any large university, including those most protective of its priorities and operations, usually acknowledge that duplication of effort, lack of planning, difficulties of coordination, and inadequate internal communication dominate institutional life. All of this creates numerous structural impediments to the realization of all university goals, educational and otherwise. It also reinforces organizational inertia and ensures an institutional resistance to change.

Bigness also ensures that considerable energy must be directed at coordinating, however inadequately, internal bureaucratic affairs. Literally thousands of memoranda are written and distributed each year at places like Berkeley and UCLA. As any insider can attest, a veritable mountain of paper is created, not all of which is intrinsically necessary or useful in accomplishing university objectives. Generating paperwork becomes an end in itself, alienated both from the real purposes of the university and from the human beings who staff the institution.

A concomitant development is the establishment of seemingly infinite numbers of committees. The massive time that university administrators and support personnel spend dealing with each other in this context rarely works to the advantage of undergraduate education. Indeed, in large universities, faculty and other educational personnel are inevitably drawn into the committee process, further eroding their time, their ability, and even their will to work closely with undergraduates. Finally, this cumbersome bureaucratic arrangement ensures that most decisions will be consensus decisions, based on political expediency, personal interest, and territorial concern. They are often far removed from what is educationally desirable, the likely result of a mechanism that usually precludes vigor, boldness, and educational vision.

Probably the worst feature of a gigantic bureaucratic organization is the pervasive impersonality hovering over all institutional activities. Any undergraduate (or anyone else) at Berkeley, UCLA, Michigan, Wisconsin, and similar multiversities has regularly felt like a character in a Kafka novel. Personal accounts of indifferent treatment and hostile reactions to reasonable requests are legion. No week goes by without bureaucratic horror stories from my students. The proverbial "runaround" is so commonplace that even the worst abuses rarely evoke surprise. Computerization has worsened the atmosphere of impersonality as programming errors and malfunctions add to the personal frustrations of students and others. Human judgment and discretion have all too often been replaced by arbitrary and mechanistic bureaucratic responses. Undergraduates in particular suffer from the excesses of this environment, since they exist at the lowest end of the entire university hierarchy of status and privilege.

Such an atmosphere guarantees a powerful psychological damper on learning in the large research university. It is bad enough that students are subjected to long lines and callous treatment in the Registrar's Office or the Financial Aid Office. Even worse - and surprisingly common - is when they encounter rudeness from professors and other instructional officials. The result is deeply anti-educational, a process of human alienation with personal and social implications far beyond one's undergraduate years. And while impersonality exists in all large systems and organizations, its presence in institutions of higher learning is especially troublesome.

Finally, the massive administrative structure of major universities attracts certain kinds of personnel who, for various reasons, are particularly ill suited for work in educational organizations. One comparatively recent development is the infusion of professional administrators into the infrastructure of academic life. Many of these men and women have been trained as professional managers, often with academic degrees and formal certifications in business and public administration. By training and temperament, these people are inclined to work in organizations without regard for the broader aims or the moral significance of the enterprise as a whole. For many, managerial advancement *per se* is the overriding aim of their activities. They have made careful career projections and scarcely take into account the broader implications of what they do on a daily basis. For all too many, academic administration is no different from any other form of management. Many, in fact, move easily from universities to governmental agencies to private corporations and other organizations seeking aggressive, upwardly mobile administrative technicians. This attitude of "pure" management, the application of financial, personnel, and related skills to any enterprise, has many consequences for education. These technocratic personalities are not especially hostile to education. Rather, they are merely indifferent to it, an attitude that may indeed be even more insidious. For the thousands of persons in this category, career advancement along these lines makes it impossible to think seriously about education and human values, much less to implement qualitative changes in this direction. Clearly, the attitudes and actions of an organization's key employees determine the values of the organization itself.

Not all university administrators are drawn from the ranks of amoral, careerist technicians. Significant numbers also emerge from the faculty, men and women who have front-line personal experience with various dimensions of teaching and undergraduate education. Some of these people, to be sure, bring a valuable perspective to their administrative responsibilities. They are able to connect their work as administrators to broader educational and other goals of the university. Some of them have occasionally slowed down the process of transforming the university into merely any other large bureaucracy, designed to perpetuate itself absent of any genuine vision or purpose.

Sadly, there are far too few of such academic administrators. Administration with vision is rare in any context, a disturbing reality that encompasses most who have emerged from faculty backgrounds. Indeed, in some troublesome ways, these persons are often motivated by inappropriate concerns. There is considerable truth to the allegation that many faculty members seek to become administrators precisely because they have tired of teaching and have been unproductive as scholars. Though it is embarrassing for universities to admit, and despite vociferous denials, there are thousands of unproductive professors. Their elevation to administrative ranks provides an honorable mechanism to keep them employed, particularly those with lifetime tenure. Many academics too who have experienced burnout seek administrative careers in order to find equivalent status and higher salaries. While not necessarily hostile to education, they do little to effect the kind of structural change necessary in light of modern educational and social problems. Many, unfortunately, become immersed in the trivia of administrative life. They get quickly infatuated with power and the petty squabbles that dominate academic affairs.

Whether drawn from academic or other sources, administrators in all large organizations tend to undergo some subtle character transformations. Academic administration is not easy; much of the work involves dealing with people who want something, a problem intensified during times of fiscal scarcity. Inevitably, this requires university administrators to reject a number of reasonable requests. The result is often a series of ill feelings and defensive attitudes that in time become harsh and mean-spirited. A culture of extreme negativity prevails today throughout the administrative structure of the modern university. This is hardly conducive to broader, more humane educational objectives.

Perhaps more significant, administrators in large hierarchies are rarely content to stay where they are. There is something apparently immutable about life in a bureaucracy that impels people to strive for advancement up a managerial ladder. Few Assistant Deans care to remain Assistant Deans and few Associate Vice Chancellors care to remain in that position. The Assistant Dean has an eye on a "real" Deanship and the Associate Vice Chancellor wants to become a full Vice Chancellor. As Kurt Vonnegut has so eloquently put it, so it goes.

Without disparaging the commendable human desire for career advancement, it is necessary to mention some of the implications of this phenomenon. Bureaucrats who are constantly on the lookout for the next position conduct their affairs in particular ways. When career moves are at stake, people act with extreme caution. Care is taken to please those with the power to determine advancement and promotion. Decisions are made by virtue of calculations in line with personal advantage. Not surprisingly, this is often at variance with genuine educational need. More important, caution and political calculation for personal ends are generally inimical to vision and boldness, qualities desperately needed in the modern university. Far too many university administrators have internalized an attitude of not rocking the boat, to the maintenance of what is at the expense of what might be. The persistence of these attitudes retards the opportunities for change and ensures the perpetuation of educational mediocrity.

It would be difficult to design a university organizational system that is less conducive to good undergraduate education. The structure of narrow academic departments combines with a vast bureaucracy to prevent the creation and implementation of genuine educational vision. This is, unfortunately, what the multiversity has become in the 1980's. Kerr's pluralist model can be little else. Notwithstanding his immensely perceptive commentary about the unfortunate implications for undergraduate students, the system itself makes it inevitable. What education does occur is random and unsystematic. It happens largely because there are some dedicated teachers and even a few sensitive administrators who struggle to reverse the tide. Without fundamental changes, however, their efforts are doomed to be haphazard, intermittent, and fraught with overwhelming frustration.

NOTES

1. Clark Kerr, *The Uses of the University* (Cambridge, Massachusetts: Harvard University Press, 1963), pp.7-8.

2. For useful accounts of academic departmentalization, see Laurence Veysey, *The Emergence of the American University* , 1965 and Frederick Rudolph, *The American College and University*, 1965.

3. This has been noted by other critical scholars. Herbert Schiller, for example, indicated the absurdity of the separation of economics and political science: "Each discipline insists on its own purity, and the models most admired in each field are

those that exclude the untidy effects of interaction with other disciplines. Economics is for economists; politics is for political scientists. Though the two are inseparable in the world of reality, academically their relationship is disavowed or disregarded." *The Mind Managers* (Boston: Beacon Press, 1973), pp.26-27.

4. Kerr, op. cit., p.44.

5. As a further example of the complexity of the administrative superstructure, the following offices exist under and report to the Registrar: Assistant Registrar for Data Processing; Assistant Registrar for Registration, Enrollment, and Scheduling; Assistant Registrar for Records; Assistant Registrar for Student Services and Degrees; Section on Course Reports (Grades); Section for Intercampus Transfer; Residence Classifications; Schedule Office; Transcripts Office; Withdrawals; Student Information Office; and several others.

6. For an excellent account of modern bureaucracy, see Ralph Hummel, *The Bureaucratic Experience*, 1977. Drawing on the pioneering work of Max Weber, Hummel shows how human relations are transformed into control relations in bureaucracies. The implications for large universities are obvious.

CHAPTER 3

On Academic Character and Personality

Who are the people serving on the faculties of the nation's most prestigious research universities? With some conspicuous exceptions, they are intelligent and accomplished scholars who hold honorable and respected positions. Like other American middle class professionals, they tend to be absorbed with their work and with their careers. Like thousands of doctors, lawyers, dentists and others, many are given to an excessive concentration on their work, sometimes to the detriment of other features of their personalities and to their relationships with other human beings. They are, by and large, acutely aware of their social status and of their broader role in society, remarkably similar to attitudes of their counterparts in comparable professional settings.

The most honest answer to the question of who the faculty members in the multiversity are is simply that they are very much like other middle class people, except that they are mostly white and mostly male. Like other reasonably affluent Americans, they own houses, they marry and have families, they go on vacations, they worry about taxes, they vote in elections, they are concerned about crime, and they have hopes and aspirations for the future. Some are very happy persons and others are not. Some have successful marriages while others seem unable to sustain personal relationships. Most are moderate in personal habits and affairs while others are alcoholics and other substance abusers. Some are decent and sensitive to waitresses and gardeners while others are abusive and condescending in their intercourse with persons of lesser social and occupational status. In short, they are extremely similar in most basic ways to their fellows of comparable social class standing and values.

This characterization would doubtless offend many professors, who want desperately to believe that they are profoundly different, superior, and unique. Academic accomplishment generates a highly developed sense of elitism, and this perspective dominates the consciousness of many thousands of university professors in the United States. The idea that they are like everyone else, save only for their expertise in their specific fields, is apparently unnerving to many of them. Perhaps in response to the hesitation to see themselves as ordinary, accomplished middle class professionals, they and the public relations apparatus of the contemporary multiversity have created an image of professors remarkably different from the reality.

What follows in this chapter is a series of reflections and observations about the character and personality of today's academics. In accordance with the methodology of the book outlined in Chapter 1, I cheerfully acknowledge that these are based on subjective observations over the years in high powered academic institutions. My remarks emerge from honest evaluations, and I frankly admit that they are both provocative and speculative, beyond the realm of empirical proof or quantitative verification. I have reluctantly come to conclude that the emotional makeup of far too many professors renders them particularly ill-suited to university level teaching, advising, and most important, service as personal role models. Certainly, this is not universal. My sole point is that enough professors are what I describe so as to have a major and deplorable influence on undergraduate education. For a variety of reasons, I believe that thousands of university professors lack not only the will to become intimately involved in the educational affairs of undergraduate students, but also lack the temperament and character to do so successfully.

Even a modest perusal of university catalogues and similar publications reveals the kind of inflated image that professors wish to promote to the external world - and, as I believe, even more to themselves. When prestigious research universities seek to attract top students, recruiters regale them with stories of Nobel Prize winners and potential opportunities to study and work closely with the finest minds in the world. Students are told that study in the university will enable them to be at the forefront of the creation of knowledge. They often leave such sessions believing that they are about to embark upon a course of study with some of the world's intellectual giants, geniuses who combine brilliant academic discoveries with a powerful commitment to teaching.

This rhetoric about Nobel Prize winners is misleading and dishonest, and students quickly discover that their instruction in the multiversity is far from exciting and engaging. They also discover that, as undergraduates, they have very little contact with Nobel Prize winners and the like. What they may never discover, or only dimly deduce, is that even in the "best" universities, there are extremely few men and women of that intellectual stature. The UCLA catalogue, for example, indicates that "The faculty of the University of California is internationally known for its distinguished academic achievements. On its nine campuses the University has 18 Nobel Laureates, and membership in the National Academy of Science is the largest of any university in the country." A page earlier, that publication notes that "UCLA's distinguished faculty includes Nobel laureates and many members of the National Academy of Science and the American Academy of Arts and Sciences [and between] 1964 and 1981, UCLA ranked sixth in the nation in the number of prestigious John Simon Guggenheim Fellowships awarded to faculty members."[1]

The blunt reality, however, is that there are many thousands of faculty members at the University of California and comparable institutions, the vast majority of whom are not Nobel winners or potential Nobel winners. They are good, even superior at what they do. They achieve impressive professional recognition for their academic efforts and accomplishments. They are generally authorities in their fields. They are highly intelligent and professionally successful. They know how to do research in their specific areas as well as most others in the world. They are among the best journeyman academics around. That they are not necessarily geniuses, however, generates a complex of personal insecurities and other emotional reactions that is dysfunctional to the educational obligations of the university. This phenomenon, not well understood and rarely discussed, is as important as the organizational structure of the multiversity in defeating the goal of adequate and humane education.

It is essential to explore this phenomenon in some depth. Before examining the emotional implications arising out of not being geniuses, it is necessary to develop this assertion more fully. Some unusually perceptive academics have already had the courage to express that conclusion with commendable candor. More than thirty years ago, C. Wright Mills painted a picture of professors dramatically different from both the public relations gloss and thousands of internal self-images:

> Men of brilliance, energy, and imagination are not often attracted to college teaching . . . It is easier to become a professor, and it is easier to continue out of inertia . . . The personable young man, willing to learn quickly the thought-ways of others, may succeed as readily or even more readily than the truly original mind in intensive contact with the world of learning . . . The specialization that is required for successful operation as a college professor is often deadening to the mind that would grasp for higher culture in the modern world . . . Such serious thought as he engages in is thought within one specialty, one groove . . . The professor of social science, for example, is not very likely to have as balanced an intellect as a top-flight journalist . . . The professionalization of knowledge has thus narrowed the grasp of the individual professor . . . in the social studies and the humanities the attempt to imitate exact science narrows the mind to microscopic fields of inquiry, rather than expanding it to embrace man and society as a whole . . . After he is established in a college, it is unlikely that the professor's milieu and resources are the kind that will facilitate, much less create, independence of mind. He is a member of a petty hierarchy, almost completely closed in by its middle-class environment . . . In such a hierarchy, mediocrity makes its own rules and sets its own image of success.[2]

Mills has not been the only prominent "insider" to notice the large gap between academic pretensions and academic reality. A century ago, in 1883, Friedrich Nietzsche realized that most of his academic colleagues were modest intellectual technicians rather than major or seminal thinkers and intellectual leaders.

In his classic, *Thus Spoke Zarathrusta*, he made the point with characteristic sarcasm:

> They are good clockworks, but take care to wind them correctly! Then they indicate the hour without fail and make a modest noise. They work like mills and like stamps: Throw down your seedcorn to them and they will know how to grind it small and reduce it to white dust.[3]

There is strong reason to believe that this phenomenon has intensified in the contemporary era. In an admirably blunt view of modern academics, Professor Andrew Hacker offered a variety of observations that begin to focus on some hidden emotional realities that pervade the modern university and that serve as powerful deterrents to sensitive and effective undergraduate education:

> The scholarly system . . . adapts itself to the needs of its members . . . A kind of collective security evolves, based on an agreement that lack of outstanding ability need not exclude an individual from gaining a respectable reputation . . . [T]he growth in academic employment has had the inevitable effect of diluting the quality of the scholarly calling. For every individual of superior intellect admitted...in recent years, several newly created places have been filled by persons of mediocre capacities. The idea that any profession can undergo so great a numerical expansion and still maintain the quality it hitherto had is [a] major illusion . . . Such sophistry can, of course, raise the esteem of those recently admitted to professional standing. It is not the first time that reality has been redefined in order to encourage self-congratulation.[4]

Academics, probably unique among middle-class professionals in America, find it difficult to accept and live within their own intellectual limitations. The vast majority of competent lawyers, for example, are perfectly content to live out their professional lives without being Clarence Darrows. Most physicians, similarly, are content to perform their professional work even with the realization that they will labor without the benefits of Nobel prizes or similar accolades. Many professors, however, seem fundamentally incapable of making a similarly mature adjustment to their personal and professional limitations.

Thousands of professors, especially those employed by prestigious multiversities, would bristle at any comparison with doctors, lawyers, dentists, and certified public accountants. They would protest that their work is fundamentally different from that of the others, whose contributions lie primarily in the mere application of a professional body of knowledge. They would urge a recognition that scholars, unlike other professionals, have the responsibility to advance the frontiers of human knowledge through their special skills as researchers and investigators.

There is no question that the raison d'etre of the modern research university is to advance knowledge through discoveries in all fields of endeavor. At the highest levels, this function is performed well and occasionally even brilliantly. But most professors - the vast majority - even at the "best" universities can never be in this category by virtue of the inevitable intellectual limitations affecting most of the human population. Instead, their efforts are competent research activities that, as I shall indicate in the next chapter, advance their personal careers for more than the boundaries and frontiers of human knowledge. They are skilled technicians much in the same mold as optometrists, engineers, pharmacists, and others. I have come to conclude that much of their activity and their attitudes are expressions of a strong desire, sometimes conscious and sometimes not, to avoid that characterization. There are profound consequences and implications arising out of avoiding - and actively denying - the reality of not being geniuses, of not really being at forefront of the intellectual world. As Hacker has suggested, reality is often redefined in order to encourage self-congratulation.

There is thus a powerful emotional foundation for the tendency of major universities to become involved in the rating game described earlier in this book. The obsessive quest for visibility and professional recognition in the modern academic world not only defeats the process of education, but it also reinforces the powerful insecurities and resentments of far too many members of the American professoriate. These insecurities and resentments pervade the daily life of the profession, and their existence and reinforcement only add additional barriers to those who would promote humane and socially beneficial reform in higher education.

These emotional realities are manifested in an extraordinary number of ways. Above all, American academics have established a complex and effective system of self-congratulation. This system has formal and informal mechanisms that both reinforce the heightened self-images of individual professors, and that prevent a serious confrontation with underlying fears and intellectual insecurities. The formal devices range from the regular processes of advancement and promotion[5] to the public relations gloss to the regular gatherings of academics in disciplinary associations and special topic conferences. In all of these activities and processes, favored academics are told orally and in writing how good they are and how important their work is to the tradition of intellectual discovery. Those who organize and control these processes know fully well that they too will intermittently be the recipients of similar praise from their academic peers.

The scholarly conference is a particularly important example of how academic men and women can formalize the public expression of mutual admiration. Conferences can and do perform entirely legitimate academic functions. They are frequently valuable for exchanging information and current research findings. They are similarly useful in generating a range of personal contacts with persons working in related fields. Clearly, research can be more effectively conducted when investigators know precisely what others are doing and the directions in which their discoveries are going. It would be foolish to deny the real value of this method of scholarly interaction and communication.

But there is also a hidden agenda, one replete with the kind of emotional significance discussed earlier. At these conventions and conferences, leading professors have the opportunity to parade in public; many veritably strut around as peacocks, showing their peers and colleagues their various intellectual feathers. They - and their lesser luminaries - take every advantage of the glowing introductions and favorable peer comments. The system of academic conferences provides a legitimization for masses of professors to tell each other how

47

wonderful they are, under a cover of scholarly discourse that conceals the more unseemly aspects of a mutual admiration society. I am convinced, after attending more than a score of these affairs in recent years, that the hidden agenda of emotional reassurance is at least as important as the formal academic and scholarly agenda. All human beings, professors no less than anyone else, require regular assurance of their worth and value as human beings. They want and need confirmation of the skill and competence of their work. My observations convince me, however, that professors take this phenomenon to an unhealthy extreme.

There are hundreds of equally insecure doctors, lawyers, engineers, and journalists. It is probably a human universal for people to seek confirmation of their abilities by creating networks for mutual admiration. There is, however, a darker side to human insecurity. In the hands of professors, this darker side has some devastating educational implications.

Inflated rhetoric about one's self-worth is a traditional reflection of human insecurity. The murkier side of this phenomenon occurs in the tendency to disparage the standing and competence of others. This finds extensive expression in the modern research university. One of the most striking features of daily academic life is the way that many professors call attention to their own superiority by reference to the inferiority of others.

I have heard these expressions of resentment and repressed envy hundreds of times during the past decade and a half, most often in private conversations in such informal settings as parties, meals, and various recreational activities. Often such comments take the form of complaints about how "mere" journalists or doctors or lawyers do not create knowledge, but rather manipulate it for their narrow professional objectives - in apparent contrast to scholars, for whom knowledge is somehow a higher, more noble proposition divorced of personal or professional advantage. The resentment towards others (and thus the emotional elevation of self) is never more dramatically manifested than in complaints about income disparities among professionals. To underscore their feelings of lack of appreciation, university professors call repeated attention to the fact that they are paid much less well, for example, than doctors or lawyers.[6] There is a virtual ritual incantation that the world neither understands nor rewards the production of scholarship and the discovery of knowledge. There is a certain emotional gratification in feeling persecuted, victimized, and unappreciated. When done in modest proportions, such feelings are generally harmless. When taken to excess, however, they can seriously interfere with broader professional obligations. Sadly, this has become just one more negative feature in the educational inadequacies of the modern university.

The extraordinary insecurity of many academic men and women is more perniciously manifested in attitudes and actions within the institution itself. The obsessive need to disparage others in order to elevate themselves encourages many academics to reinforce already rigid hierarchies within the multiversity. Non-academics (and "inferior" classes of academics) are too often treated with condescension and even contempt. Clerical workers in particular[7] suffer the brunt of these attitudes and actions. Two recent examples are instructive in showing just how pervasive this phenomenon is and how it impedes and defeats the articulated objectives of higher education. In one case, a full professor at UCLA serving as the principal investigator on a computer based development project was asked to confer and consult with the chief programmer. Incensed and humiliated at the possibility of having to defer in a substantive matter to a subordinate, he refused, remarking that the programmer had merely a B.A. degree, while he, the professor, had a Ph.D. This is hardly an isolated example. The cult of the Ph.D. has reached immense proportions in the multiversity, creating an atmosphere that is as destructive of human relationships as it is of the educational mission of the institution.

In another instance, a course proposal dealing with neuroscience was submitted for approval to the UCLA Academic Senate Committee on Undergraduate Courses and Curricula. In this instance, the faculty member in charge of the course was a full professor in the School of Dentistry. When the course committee received the proposal, immediate questions were raised. As the head of the program under which the course was organized and taught, I was telephoned by the committee chair. He told me that some of the committee members had reservations about a dentist teaching a course

49

dealing with neuroscience. The tone of the conversation was revealing. It was obvious that the professor in the Dental School was considered an intellectual inferior, by virtue of his possession of the D.D.S. degree. When I informed the committee that he also held a Ph.D. in neuroscience, the matter was quickly resolved. While it is appropriate for a course committee to examine the academic qualifications of an instructor, what occurred here went considerably beyond this function. Instead, it was yet another example of collegial disparagement, an expression of the need of some research professors validating their own worth by reducing that of another. In this case, once again, it was a "mere" dentist probably commanding a significantly larger salary. Such an environment can scarcely be conducive to the kind of peer cooperation that can lend itself to an effective instructional program.

Perhaps the most insidious expression of this immature emotional phenomenon occurs when orthodox research professors malign their students and their colleagues who happen to be effective and sensitive teachers - especially those teachers with the temerity to cross the disciplinary boundaries of the multiversity. It is commonplace in all educational institutions to make fun of students. They are, after all, generally poorly informed, not well read, deficient in analytic and verbal skills, and often tremendously immature and self-centered. They are sometimes tempting targets for satire. In the privacy of personal conversations among teachers, such expression when done in moderation is neither harmful nor unethical. It is a legitimate and at times cathartic release from the inevitable frustrations of professional life.

At large and prestigious research universities, however, this phenomenon too often transcends moderation. It is the same expression of that powerful sense of resentment and insecurity that pollutes the academic atmosphere. I have heard, many hundreds of times over the years, my colleagues talk harshly and even bitterly about their students. Their remarks revolve around the intellectual unworthiness of their students, their sheer stupidity, their unshakable ignorance, and, above all, their lack of appreciation of the scholarly enterprise. There is often meanness and cruelty in this private invective, an attitude that clearly can only exacerbate the normal tensions between teachers and students. It takes little genius to conclude that the cause of education is ill served under these circumstances. University teachers need not love their student constituencies, nor do they necessarily need to establish close personal relationships with them in order to perform effectively as educators. But there must be a basic modicum of respect for students. Regrettably, a dangerously large percentage of contemporary professors seem emotionally incapable of such consciousness.

Sniping at colleagues who are outstanding and popular teachers is probably the most damaging and tragic feature of modern higher education. One of the most brutal ironies of university life today is the recognition that to develop a reputation as an excellent teacher is professionally disadvantageous and dangerous. In 1974, I experienced this in shocking fashion at Berkeley. When I was nominated for an Academic Senate Distinguished Teacher Award, I was warned by sympathetic senior colleagues that I should withdraw from the competition, lest I become identified as a "mere" teacher rather than as a productive scholar. Such warnings were not facetious; my faculty friends knew well the attitudes and underlying emotions of many of their fellow professors.

It is disgracefully common for university professors to feel contempt for and express suspicions about good teachers who are widely respected by undergraduate students. A regular, even relentless refrain is that these teachers seek student popularity in order to compensate for their own inadequacies as researchers. Allegations of showmanship abound, with the suggestion that mere entertainment has been substituted for genuinely rigorous academic preparation. Furthermore, popular teachers are regularly accused (most often privately, occasionally publicly) of seeking to gather groups of uncritical student sycophants around them. The implication is that popular teachers are in essence frauds, men and women who are beyond the pale of respected academic life. To outsiders, this must seem bizarre, an attitude that mocks the ostensible purpose of higher education. I can only confirm, however, that such attitudes are ubiquitous.

It is worthwhile to explore the emotional sources of these harmful and irrational values and attitudes. Why is there such hostility towards those faculty members who have achieved

51

great popularity among students and for whom such reactions are sources of personal pride and professional gratification? In major research universities, faculty members are selected among persons who are often more comfortable in the library or laboratory than they are in personal interactions, especially with undergraduate students. Thousands of students often report difficulties in communicating with such professors, especially if the subject matter transcends specific course content. It seems apparent, therefore, that there is enormous envy and jealousy for those professors who create close teacher-student relationships. A harsh but obvious explanation for such widespread hostility is that many professors resent a form of personal education of which they are profoundly incapable.

This same psychological phenomenon is frequently manifested in similar hostility towards faculty members who refuse to be shackled by the arbitrary and educationally dysfuntional boundaries of academic disciplines. These academic mavericks have violated the informal rules of propriety in the research multiversity. Attacks upon them by their more cautious and conventional colleagues reveal both some important underlying emotional realities and basic institutional drives toward orthodoxy and conformity.

At prestigious research universities, many faculty members appear unusually defensive about their academic specializations and research. They often seem threatened by educational activities that depart from their own training and disciplinary outlook. These personality variables play a powerful role at universities like Berkeley and UCLA and have enormous political significance throughout the world of higher education.

Intellectual synthesis and interdisciplinary education apparently are disconcerting enterprises to large numbers of research-oriented academics. The identities of many university professors revolve heavily around their academic specializations. Like most professional people, they acquire a strong emotional interest in their work. Similarly, they develop strategies, often unconsciously, to rationalize their basic activities and values. A concomitant effect is the development of defensive attitudes towards those whose educational and scholarly outlooks proceed on different assumptions.

52

The implications of these natural processes are sometimes striking. At large research universities, status and professional recognition, as detailed earlier in this book, depend on expertise and publication in specific academic fields. In practice, this means production in relatively narrow sub-areas of knowledge. Professors already trained as graduate students in a culture of extreme and even absurd specialization adopt easily to this norm. Such powerful socialization is quickly internalized, with significant emotional consequences. For many academics, greater academic breadth - a perspective infinitely more valuable to the vast majority of undergraduate students - is outside their ken, and therefore subject to a priori rejection.

Mere rejection would be bad enough, for it would contribute to a stultifying environment of orthodoxy on a university campus. Even worse are the regular harsh verbal attacks of traditional scholars on interdisciplinary colleagues. Such attacks are powerful reflections of the emotional realities of defensiveness and resentment. They frequently mask profound feelings of personal inadequacy. Regularly, interdisciplinary teachers are accused of being amateurs and dilettantes, who ignore scholarly traditions and academic rigor. Allegations of complicity in reducing academic standards may indeed be attempts to convince themselves of the value of their own intellectual work and contributions. While psychological variables cannot explain the totality of faculty hostility to the broader intellectual perspectives of interdisciplinary education, their importance cannot be ignored.

The excessive way that professors' lives revolve around their narrow academic interests is decidedly unhealthy for higher education. It is perfectly understandable, of course, that an academic who spends his or her professional life around a specific subject area should acquire a powerful emotional interest in that area. There is nothing especially unusual, in fact, about persons wishing to justify the basic patterns of their life's activities. It only becomes personally and socially troublesome when this natural phenomenon becomes so strong that it reduces tolerance and discourages respect for human differences. Throughout major universities today, serious intellectual speculation and most proposals for educational change and reform are discouraged, because they pose a severe personal and emotional threat to thousands of university professors. It may well be a human universal to view anything different with fear and anxiety. Such feelings, however natural, cannot be advantageous in an institution purportedly dedicated to the free and open expression of ideas - including those that differ radically from those whose influence dominates institutional life. Extreme emotional identification with an academic field or sub-field tends to reduce intellectual adaptability and flexibility, qualities desperately necessary if today's students are to deal adequately with the transdisciplinary problems of the 21st century.

A more general analysis of academic character and personality is revealing in explaining the wide gap between the theoretical potential of university life and its actual performance. It is well to inquire into the kinds of people who, with surprisingly rare exceptions, are selected for positions at the nation's premier research universities. As I shall show, this selection process works to the profound disadvantage of undergraduate university education. The phenomenon is neither malicious nor conspiratorial; human beings in all organizations select those who are compatible in social class, educational background, values, temperament, and a wide variety of more subtle personality factors. Faculty selections are perfectly rational within this framework. For reasons that will become obvious, however, the framework itself stands in dire need of adjustment and correction.

Men and women who have been academically successful their entire lives, with few exceptions, dominate academic life in the major research institutions in the United States. At first blush, this seems perfectly natural and appropriate, for it is obvious that academic organizations should be populated by people who have been highly proficient in that enterprise. Not even the most radical critic of modern higher education would argue that universities should be run by persons without impressive scholarly accomplishments and credentials. Clearly, people who do well in academic pursuits belong as faculty members in modern universities.

Further reflection, however, reveals that this issue is far from simple. It is appropriate to inquire much more deeply into what really constitutes academic success and into the character and personalities of those people who rise to the top in the present system of education at all levels in America. What kinds of people typically do well in school, progressing as they do from elementary school to secondary school to undergraduate studies to graduate work?

The process of academic "success" begins very early. Assuredly, it involves high intelligence, for without that quality, serious and sustained academic work is plainly impossible. But equally important, it requires great persistence, the ability to persevere in the face of all academic assignments, those that are trivial and pedantic no less than those that are serious and substantial. Indeed, this latter quality is crucial at all levels of education. It elevates the choice for positive recognition from teacher-superiors from as early as kindergarten to as late as the final draft of the doctoral dissertation. Most important of all in the quest for academic success is the personal capacity and propensity for adjustment. Boys or girls, and later men and women, who adjust well and conform easily to authority elevate their opportunities for recognition by those in positions to provide both personal encouragement and formal recommendations to the next level of the educational system. A premium exists, therefore for those who combine intelligence with the capacity to please those in positions of power and authority. As I shall indicate shortly, such persons are hardly the most valuable people to be employed as educators in American colleges and universities.

The people who "do the best" in school are not necessarily the most intelligent. Most important, they are rarely the most creative and imaginative. Quite the contrary - boys and girls who combine intelligence with character, imagination, and personal will often find the formal process of schooling to be stultifying and repressive - an institutional arrangement that promotes sterile conformity over boldness and intellectual risk-taking. No matter how intelligent and perceptive, those whose temperaments incline them to adapt to the values and ideas of others are unlikely to be seriously original thinkers in their own right. Instead, whether wittingly or not, they become in time purveyors of new orthodoxies, inflicting on their students the same process that has been inflicted on them in earlier years. This mind-set is little short of pernicious, and a central tragedy of modern university life is that it goes so profoundly unrecognized. A large majority of university faculty members fall into that category - men and women who have become veritable masters of adjustment and who insist on equally servile responses from the people now beholden to them in the academic hierarchy.

The influence of graduate school is immensely significant in this educationally dubious process of professional socialization. C. Wright Mills was remarkably perceptive thirty years ago in his characterization of the graduate school as a feudal entity encouraging high level intellectual conformity. An even harsher judgment would hardly be inappropriate. Far too much of contemporary graduate work leading to the Ph.D. degree involves significant activity approaching a state of intellectual prostitution. Thousands of past and present graduate students, in pursuit of advanced degrees required for certification to academic legitimacy, have found it expedient to conform to the academic ideology of their professor-superiors. What is, originally, tactically advantageous soon becomes emotionally and politically necessary, and the junior initiates quickly become eager proselytes of the prevailing orthodoxy. This process inexorably alters consciousness. Over the period of graduate education, often extending to six or seven years or more, the kind of peonage, deference, and sheer servility required for success becomes internalized. The personality implications go beyond one's academic work and pervade the entirety of one's life.

The general public usually fails to realize that graduate studies are often an artificially prolonged period of adolescence. The problem is that many graduate students are men and women in their late 20's and even their 30's - an age in which their contemporaries are generally well established in careers and in other activities characteristic of maturity and adulthood. This extension of a period of life in which persons are neither children nor adults inevitably takes a psychic toll. And while there are exceptions, most of the people who emerge from this process harbor deep resentments and hostilities that are expressed in their own work as teachers. Like fraternity members who have been subjected to the humiliations of hazing, far too many professors appear eager to have their own turn in the dominant role of a master-slave relationship.

Naturally, large numbers of graduate students never complete the arduous process of finishing the Ph.D. Some, of course, cannot complete the course of study because of a wide range of academic deficiencies. Many, however, voluntarily leave their graduate studies, because they are unwilling to subject themselves to the torments of prolonged adolescence and professional servility. Many in this category also decline to conform intellectually to whatever academic approach or style happens to be demanded at the time. Ironically, many of the Ph.D. drop-outs are far more emotionally suited for university faculty careers than their more ostensibly successful peers who complete the doctoral process. They have displayed those qualities of independence, character, and maturity that would be far more valuable for undergraduate students (as well as for the production and discovery of knowledge) than the opposite qualities of dependence, adjustment, hostility, resentment, and displaced aggression.

The successful survivors of this lengthy process of formal education often display other personality characteristics that detract from their daily responsibilities as undergraduate educators. It is well to recall that many university professors have spent virtually their entire lives in school, with one year of kindergarten, twelve years of elementary, junior high, and high school, four years of undergraduate work, and seven or eight years of graduate study. This amounts to a quarter-century of student life. Many of these persons who have done spectacularly well in this arena have done very little else with their lives.

It is no exaggeration to note that many accomplished scholars serving on university faculties are not widely experienced in those aspects of life that go beyond the domain of books, libraries, laboratories, and other features of the scholarly enterprise. Many find themselves uncomfortable with the more prosaic features of daily existence with which most people learn to grapple at an early age. Except in extremely abstract terms, many professors are unfamiliar with (and often arrogantly uninterested in) vast areas of human activity. Their fundamental lack of contact with the world, save for its narrow academic component, ill equips them to serve as teachers to undergraduate university students. Academics who are largely ignorant of many of the complexities of human living are in a bad position to assist students, the overwhelming majority of whom will be involved in the mainstream of social and commercial life - and who will not become Ph.D.'s in academic disciplines. One of the most pressing responsibilities of higher education in the final decades of the 20th century is to connect knowledge with life. Those who by temperament and training cannot do this effectively are apt to be poor teachers and advisors and even poorer role models.

Insular, excessively bookish existences unfortunately generate even greater problems for students in modern research universities. Far too many professors are extremely ill at ease even in the mundane aspects of human communication. Scholars quite often seek the solace and refuge of academic life precisely in order to avoid dealing closely with other people. Thousands of students can attest to awkward and strained interactions with their professors. In my own experience as a university teacher, I have spoken regularly to students who report that their professors were unable to sustain even a five or ten minute conversation. I have heard vivid accounts of professors who avoid eye contact, who shake and twitch, and who in numerous non-verbal ways, make it abundantly clear that they seek to discourage out-of-class contact with their students. In one extreme case, a colleague reports of one professor at a prestigious university whose nervousness in social intercourse is so intense that he can only respond to student questions in writing. The implications for serious education under these circumstances are both obvious and horrendous.

In one of the most revealing conversations in my academic career, I had occasion to speak to a well respected, highly orthodox professor at Berkeley, a man who is himself an unusual combination of excellent teacher and high level academic administrator. At a cocktail party, he and I were discussing some of the problems besetting higher education, particularly some of the difficulties in the area of undergraduate teaching. In response to my comment that most Berkeley professors were mediocre teachers or worse, he readily concurred. Pointedly, he told me that this was inevitable, since a large number of Berkeley professors were men and women who were excellent scholars but otherwise emotionally crippled, especially in regard to their interactions with students. In candid, off-the-record conversations throughout academic life, the reality of his provocative assertion is frequently acknowledged.

If a disturbing percentage of university faculty members are unable to communicate effectively with their undergraduate students, another large percentage might also be viewed as overly eager to thrive on the power struggles and intra-office political intrigues that are universal features of organizational life. Universities promote a public image of a deep and abiding commitment to knowledge, an institution above the strife and pettiness of lesser entities devoted to inferior goals. Such an image is nonsense; universities are rife with squabbles and conflicts. Jobs, careers, and reputations are regularly at stake in these struggles, and the levels of meanness and brutality clearly rival that of large governmental bureaucracies or industrial corporations. Academic strife is debilitating and degrading and in every academic institution lives have been shattered and human bitterness abounds.

This is the human condition. Organizational brutality is ubiquitous, and no one who has worked has ever been able to avoid contact with this disagreeable phenomenon. Many academics, however, seem to thrive perversely in this atmosphere, often to the point that it begins to dominate much of their professional and personal lives. In his inimitably perceptive way, Nietzsche recognized this phenomenon in his own academic career over a century ago:

> They watch each other closely and mistrustfully. Inventive in petty cleverness, they want for those whose knowledge walks on lame feet: like spiders they wait. I have always seen them carefully preparing poison; and they always put on gloves of glass to do it. They also know how to play with loaded dice; and I have seen them play so eagerly that they sweated.[8]

Why does it happen that so many professors with doctoral degrees, comfortable incomes, secure employment, national and international reputations, and enviable lifestyles immerse themselves in such activity?

There are several reasons. Perhaps most important, people who are incapable of rational and sensitive communication with others (professors no less than doctors, lawyers, firemen, and clerks) rely on duplicity and intimidation in order to compensate for their emotional inadequacies. In all organizations, there are human beings who have neither the

59

ability nor the inclination to resolve conflicts and solve personal problems through open discussion, mutual respect, and sensible compromise. Instead, they become obsessed with the Machiavellian machinations of office politics. Attempts to secure personal advantages, remove personal opponents from influence and even jobs, forge empires and personal alliances, and make complicated political deals have little to do with the ostensible ends of any organization, whether corporate, governmental, or educational. Instead, they become ends in themselves and reflections of major personality problems and emotional immaturities in the participants in these intrigues. The point is that universities are not immune from these disgraceful activities and attitudes. The tragic result, once again, is a diminution in the delivery and quality of educational services as well as in all the other activities associated with modern university life.

There is perhaps another reason for the particular propensity of many academics to engage in mean and petty forms of backstabbing and human manipulation. Lying, deceit, and treachery, tactics ordinarily associated with political life in national and international affairs, are far from rare in academic politics. For many years I have wondered why professors spend such enormous time and energy on internal political activity that, beyond the personal level, has virtually no impact on anything important. I can only speculate that another feature of resentment and repressed envy is in operation. Many professors, impressed as they are with their own brilliance and intellectual standing, feel deeply aggrieved that they are so unappreciated by the general public. They believe instead that they should be included in the high councils of political power, that their wisdom qualifies them to provide advice and pass judgment on the major issues of public policy. Many envision themselves as modern versions of Plato's philosopher-king. In order to compensate for the dramatic gap between their own self-images and widespread public indifference, they turn instead, often ferociously, to the more mundane but equally Byzantine politics of academic life. This displacement both reflects and feeds some powerful and deep-seated psychic needs and serves to deflect ever greater attention from the academic mission of higher education.

Throughout this process of internal intrigue, there are winners and losers, even though beyond the personal level the stakes are pitifully low. Any insider in the university (just as any insider in any organization) has observed how men and women have been displaced from positions of responsibility, have lost their jobs, or have suffered the usual indignities of diminished status and political defeat. This too is the human condition. In the academic world, however, the process is generally accompanied by shrewd and clever rationalizations and a verbal cover that conceals the baser personal motivations that characterize office politics and intra-organizational conflicts.

In many agencies and companies, people are reasonably candid, at least in private, about their personal ambitions and negative feelings about fellow employees. When they have been successful in a political attempt to outflank or remove a personal rival, they often gloat about their political acumen and the advantages that will accrue to them as a result of their successful political maneuvers. In my experience, there is considerably less candor in university settings. Academics, skilled as they are in verbal manipulation and semantic acrobatics, are more prone to invent high and noble purposes for their descents into personal brutality and human duplicity.

Most professors would find it unseemly to perceive themselves in the same mold as anyone else with vulgar career ambitions, needs for personal domination, and quests for territorial control. Emotionally, the answer is to repress such a realization by reinforcing a mythological view of themselves as the guardians of intellectual excellence. When senior professors, for example, conspire to terminate the employment of untenured junior colleagues, it is never done to get rid of people who fail to fit in because of personality differences, lack of deferential attitudes, failure to conform to a local scholarly orthodoxy, or even intellectual superiority that is threatening to senior departmental personnel; rather, it is done in order to preserve "high intellectual standards" and "excellence." This latter term is perhaps the most overused and abused term in modern university parlance. It is employed repeatedly as an excuse to impede, hurt, and even destroy the careers of people who for whatever reasons are out of favor in the power conflicts of university life. Unlike their counterparts in business, government, and the professions, academics like to believe that their own hatchet work is really a noble expression of humane values and even a spirited but unappreciated defense of Western civilization.

Over the years I have observed one other feature of academic personality and character that constitutes a powerful impediment to effective education and academic reform. An awesome fearfulness pervades the university, especially in times of severe fiscal constraint and economic decline and instability. University professors, despite a level of job security virtually unmatched in other employment relationships, appear to be among the most timid and frightened of middle-class professionals. In both public pronouncements and private conversations, they reveal their deep nervousness about what may happen to them and occasionally even their terror at the future. Such subjective attitudes are rarely supported by objective social, economic, and political realities, even in times of significant financial distress as in the late 1970's and early 1980's. University administrators, eager to keep their faculties docile and noncombative, both exploit and intensify this state of fear and anxiety. Beyond this realm of institutional political expediency, the widespread existence of these attitudes of timidity and apprehension have severely negative implications for university operations. Men and women who live in perpetual fear are fundamentally disinclined to seek change at any level. Tormented by visions of shattered future lives, they cling with desperation to the status quo. Ironically, these attitudes serve as among the most effective barriers to even the contemplation, much less the implementation, of structural changes in the direction of improved undergraduate education.

Massive fearfulness not only discourages needed reform, but it also erodes any genuine sense of moral responsibility. Men and women who feel permanently insecure are less apt to take controversial moral stands or to speak out in the face of the daily injustices they observe throughout university affairs. Many university professors, including those with lifetime tenure, are well aware that undergraduate students are regularly ill-served and that some faculty and staff members are poorly treated or even dismissed because of institutional capriciousness rather than personal incompetence or misconduct. They know too that organized or even individual resistance to these dubious activities is morally compelled. That so many professors do not get involved when clearly they should know better is a profound indictment of the academic profession as a whole.

In the previous chapter, I examined the role and impact of a large and uncontrollable bureaucracy, with special emphasis on how the cumbersome administrative structure of the contemporary multiversity defeats the enumerated goals of educational excellence. In substantial part, this occurs because academic administration is populated by manipulative and effective career schemers who are motivated far more by personal ambition and power than by principles of educational decency. This central fact, even more than their specific personality characteristics, constitutes the major impediment to educational reform.

Still, there are certain features of the bureaucratic temperament worthy of analytic scrutiny and public exposure. Like bureaucrats everywhere, university administrators are fearful of publicity and external exposure, sometimes to seemingly pathological proportions. External knowledge of internal operations would be annoying and occasionally even embarrassing. More basically, such knowledge would dilute a major source of internal political power, the ability to control and manipulate information in directions compatible with political and personal advantage. And ever since the turmoil of the 1960's, when university affairs were commonly reported in the news media, university administrators are particularly sensitive to the dangers of widespread publicity.

This is little different from the attitudes of high-ranking managers in other organizations. All bureaucrats want to be left alone to perform their functions and plan their advancements without interference. University managers are virtually identical to their counterparts elsewhere in that respect. In due course and with the passage of time, however, this fear of publicity can get obsessive. Administrators begin to spend increasing amounts of time scheming to prevent publicity and to contain internal conflicts. Their own prospects for advancement, after all, depend on their success in containing problems quietly and effectively. The persistence of these attitudes help to create and then sustain an institutional conservatism that discourages change in every feature of internal operations. It also alters and distorts human communication within organizational settings. Conversations with Deans, Directors, Vice Chancellors and the like are invariably filtered through the lens of internal political consequence and personal advantage. None of this encourages those who would strengthen the priority of education within the overall scheme of university affairs.

One other prominent feature of the administrative temperament requires brief attention. All large organizations, universities as well as any other, spawn a class of people, usually low and middle level subordinates, who are comfortable only when rules are explicit, where procedures are settled, and where exceptions are virtually non-existent. Those who display this bureaucratic mentality abound in large research universities. Their influence is powerful and pervasive. Their cumulative effect is to impede change at every level and to pollute many of the daily activities of university life. Examples are legion, and virtually no student in a large university can avoid the immense frustration of encounters with hostile and unpleasant administrators. They are men and women with a clerk mentality for whom the prospect of creating a precedent resembles a major life crisis.

In 1983, I encountered a striking personal example of this phenomenon, one of many during my academic career. In conjunction with academic colleagues throughout the UCLA campus, I decided to assist in organizing a small seminar on nuclear war for freshman and sophomore undergraduates. In order to achieve maximum educational value and to cover some of the enormous complexities of this extremely important topic, we decided to rely on the expertise of faculty members in several areas - psychiatry, radiology, humanities, political science, and other fields. The course proposal was developed, guest speakers were obtained, and approval was granted by the undergraduate course committee of the Academic Senate. The seminar was duly scheduled for Spring term, 1983. The primary organizer of the course, a professor in the Department of Radiation Oncology in the School of Medicine, became the instructor of record, an administrative requirement for all courses throughout the university.

Shortly before the commencement of the seminar, I received a telephone call from the Schedule Office. As head of the undergraduate program with the administrative responsibility for organizing this course, I took care of all the internal administrative requirements for getting it ready for its student

64

audience. The official in the Schedule Office informed me that the course could not proceed as intended. She noted that our designated course number for this seminar, Radiation Oncology 98, was unacceptable. When I inquired as to why this was so, she told me that the Department of Radiation Oncology in the Medical School only offers graduate level instruction, indeed generally only post-M.D. instruction. And since the schedule office computer was not programmed for a graduate department offering an undergraduate course, the course could not be offered. My protestations that ends and means had been absurdly confused here fell on deaf ears, yet another victim of a bureaucratic mind-set that has negatively transformed academic priorities in the modern research university.[9]

The attitudes, personalities, and temperaments of university professors combine with the narrow mentalities of academic managers and their bureaucratic operatives to ensure a marginal status for and miniscule commitment to educational excellence. The vast complex of personal insecurities, resentments, and ambitions utterly dominates the affairs of many contemporary institutions of higher learning. These psychological forces are neither widely understood by the public nor properly appreciated even by internal critics of university priorities. When these issues are raised at all, they are quickly dismissed and often vigorously denied. Ironically, the very vehemence of these denials often serves to confirm the existence and the persistence of human emotions and motivations that belie the noble purposes that are supposed to characterize the lives and attitudes of university personnel. Only when the public, however, can pierce the veil of this inflated rhetoric will there be any chance to analyze accurately what is deficient with university operations. Then - and only then - will it be possible to formulate and implement superior selection criteria for the people who will run the institutions of higher education and provide the instructional services to the hundreds of thousands of young people who enroll each year in American research universities.

NOTES

1. UCLA General Catalogue, 1985-86, pp.4-5

2. C. Wright Mills, *White Collar* (New York: Oxford University Press, 1953), pp.130-131.

3. Friedrich Nietzsche, *Thus Spoke Zarathrustra* , p.237, in Walter Kaufmann, editor, *The Portable Nietzsche* (New York: The Viking Press, 1954).

4. Andrew Hacker, *The End of the American Era* (New York: Atheneum, 1970), pp.196-198.

5. For those not in the fold, this process can be devastating. See the next chapter on promotion and tenure.

6. I should hasten to add that such complaints are sometimes entirely justified. At the same time, professors rarely realize just how privileged they are. Few persons, for example, have such unfettered flexibility of their own time obligations.

7. This phenomenon is treated in depth in Chapter 5.

8. Nietzsche, op. cit., pp.237-238.

9. After considerable effort, this particular problem was solved; the course was in fact taught as planned.

CHAPTER 4

Maintaining the Guild: Academic Promotion and Tenure

All large organizations create mechanisms for self-preservation and perpetuation. Human beings in positions of power everywhere seek to employ, retain, and promote those men and women who share the major goals and values of organizational life. They also seek to attract and retain those who share a basic temperamental compatibility. All organizations similarly desire personnel who are competent and efficient and who are unlikely to cause friction, generate problems, or become dissident voices. Procedures to accomplish these organizational demands are often complex and specific. In virtually all white collar settings, promotion criteria constitute the kinds of hurdles that will ensure that the "right" people make it through and that the "wrong" people are filtered out. Almost always, these mechanisms are accompanied by formal and informal rhetoric that calls attention to high standards, to excellence, to productivity, and to other ideals to which the organizations are ostensibly dedicated.

Large research universities conduct their promotion activities in identical fashion. Although there are some profound differences in articulated goals, multiversities too seek people who will fit in nicely, who will perform admirably, who will enhance institutional reputations (and, increasingly, bring in substantial extramural funding), and who will minimize problems for key academic and administrative personnel in the institution. There is, however, one powerful difference. In universities (and in almost every American institution of higher learning),[1] professors who make it through the rigorous promotion process are awarded tenure, a status that guarantees a lifetime of employment in the absence of misconduct or gross incompetence. Thus the stakes in academic promotion are enormously high, for no other profession or institution except the federal judiciary awards its successful employees the guarantee of a job for the rest of their working lives.[2]

Neither the general public nor the vast majority of university undergraduates have more than a vague sense about what tenure really is, how one manages to obtain it, and what its institutional and social consequences are. This process is utterly central to higher education. Probably no feature of university life is more important than the process of promotion leading to a tenured faculty appointment. To note that tenure is highly coveted, especially in a rapidly declining academic job market, is a colossal understatement. For untenured Assistant Professors, literally nothing is more important. The aspiration to make it combines with the fear of failure to color almost totally the consciousness of these junior academic personnel.

Promotion leading to tenure, therefore, determines the very character of institutional life. Who gets promoted and retained and who does not influences the nature of research, education, and every other function performed in the modern university. It is therefore of vital significance to understand this process, to evaluate its impact, and to examine the gaps between the stated purposes of academic promotion and its actual operations and goals.

The formal objective of academic tenure is the preservation of academic freedom. In principle, academic institutions provide substantial economic and employment security to professors of demonstrable academic quality who have passed a probationary period of service. The reason for granting such security is that academic work in particular needs protection from the vicissitudes of external social and political pressures. Professors with controversial views would be reluctant to express them in class and in print unless they could have assurance that no adverse employment consequences would result from such expression. Tenure, therefore, frees professors to do what they are inclined to do, which contributes to the spirit of free inquiry in an academic environment.

Anyone even modestly conversant with the history of American higher education knows that academic freedom has come under constant and sometimes brutal attack. Throughout the twentieth century, many academics have been subject to external abuse or worse as a result of opinions they held and expressed. From the hysteria of the Palmer raids to the dark pall of McCarthyism and the Cold War to the immoralities and illegalities of the Nixon era, external powers have regularly sought to obtain the dismissals of unfavored and unpopular college and university professors. In recent years, the American Legion has mounted an assault on many instructors whose view of patriotism differs from that of the Legion. Unquestionably, without the protection of tenure, many of the intended victims of these disgraceful witchhunts would have been exposed to severe personal jeopardy.

There is another, more subtle area in which the institution of tenure serves to protect academic freedom. The employment security afforded by tenure also protects academics with unusual views or unorthodox values from internal opponents. In American universities, there are hundreds of tenured men and women who, for various reasons, see the world differently from their academic colleagues. Some have become political activists; others have departed from accepted modes of research and publication, and have addressed their written work towards the general public rather than towards fellow professors; still others have become vocal critics of specific university policies or specific university administrators, or have uttered comments more basically critical of contemporary higher education. I know people in all these categories very closely, and I know equally well that without the protection of tenure, their employment on university faculties would be highly problematic.

Not even the most intransigent defender of the tenure system, however, would assert that the sole rationale for tenure is the preservation of academic freedom. The vast majority of senior university administrators and tenured professors defend the system on the ground that it is the best guarantee of scholarly accomplishment and excellence. Tenure needs to be available to junior academic personnel in order to generate incentives for academic productivity. It supposedly ensures that the best research will be encouraged and that the best young academic minds will infuse the institution with "fresh blood." Thus the rationale for the tenure system is a complex combination of factors embracing academic freedom, employment security, and the very academic values of the institution. Indeed, tenure is so fundamental a feature of contemporary academic existence that it has become an intimate part of its folklore and culture. As Robert Nisbet has suggested, "[t]enure in the Academy is more than economic security. It cannot even be understood in economic terms. One would have to go to the realm of religion for its exact counterpart in its blend of mystique and the sacred."[3]

There is little doubt that tenure will remain a mainstay of modern university life. There are strong and passionately presented arguments for and against tenure, both of which make intelligent and persuasive points. The issue is complex and ambiguous, but the arguments are largely matters of abstract reflection and thought. This chapter assumes the maintenance of the tenure system and instead will seek to describe the ends to which it is actually employed. In addition, it will examine how the formal criteria for academic promotion and tenure often depart, at times dramatically, from the actual operational criteria. The major thesis of this chapter is that the overriding purpose of university promotion practices is to socialize academic personnel into the dominant values and priorities of the institution. I shall argue in the following pages that promotion policies have become very sophisticated devices by which the research function is advanced and by which teaching and other educational activities are fundamentally devalued. I shall show how these processes are manipulated so as to virtually ensure that only certain kinds of intellectual products can qualify a junior faculty member for promotion, while others, more suited to the educational needs of undergraduates, are quickly discouraged.

Almost all major research universities have enunciated similar policies on promotion and tenure. Usually codified in formal university documents and in faculty manuals presented to newly appointed regular[4] academic personnel, the criteria for academic advancement are virtually identical throughout the nation. The formal standards by which an Assistant Professor is evaluated for possible advancement to tenure (usually but not always to the rank of Associate Professor) involve accomplishments in several areas such as teaching, research or creative production, community or public service, and university service. The standards and policies of the University of California are commonplace:

> The review committee shall judge the candidate with respect to the proposed rank and duties, considering the record of his performance in (a) teaching, (b) research or other creative work, (c) professional activity, and (d) university and public service. In evaluating the candidate's qualifications within these areas, the review committee shall exercise reasonable flexibility, balancing where the case requires, heavier commitments in one area against lighter commitments and responsibilities in another.

A brief review of the general promotion process is a useful preface to a specific examination and critique of its actual operations. Typically, a university department will conduct a mid-term review of a professor by appointing a confidential review committee of senior departmental colleagues.[5] These senior professors convene and evaluate the professor's accomplishments and future prospects. They are charged with making a recommendation for or against promotion on the basis of the official university criteria as listed above. The first such evaluation is usually a preliminary promotion determination prior to a subsequent decision for or against tenure.

In principle, teaching and research are the most important areas and each is supposed to be evaluated equally in determining whether promotion should be granted. By general consensus and practice, subsequent reviews, with higher career stakes, proceed similarly. The other categories, while important in specific cases, are decidedly subordinate in the overall evaluation of university faculty members. Operating within this general framework, the review committee members typically report their findings and recommendations to the Chairperson of the Department. Often, this recommendation is submitted to the senior professors for a final Departmental vote. The Chairperson, in turn, reports the results to the university administration, sometimes appending any personal observations bearing upon the case. At this juncture, the file is often received by the head of the larger academic unit of which the Department is a part. Depending on the specific institution, this could be a Dean of Humanities, Social Science, Life Science, or Physical Science or it could be a Dean or Provost of a large College of Letters and Science, usually the major liberal arts entity within the multiversity structure. The designated Dean appends his or her own opinion (or, in some universities, has specific veto authority that can terminate the process at that juncture) and forwards the entire file to a general university promotion review committee. This committee, often the most powerful and prestigious faculty body on campus, often appoints a select ad hoc committee to review each faculty promotion case. Their judgment is usually determinative, and the recommendation is sent to the office of a high university official, such as a Chancellor, a President, a Vice-Chancellor for Faculty Affairs, or the like. Often the recommendation, for or against promotion (either with or without tenure depending on the particular stage of a professor's service) is approved here on a pro forma basis, although unusual or controversial cases can evoke intervention at the highest administrative levels. The specific procedures, of course, vary from institution to institution; in general, however, the promotion review process is complex and multi-layered, purportedly to ensure the highest level of rigorous peer review and quality control.

In theory, therefore, a faculty member gets promoted and eventually receives tenure by compiling an outstanding record in both teaching and research. As in life generally, however, theory and practice often diverge dramatically. It is important to recall that the massive research orientation of the contemporary multiversity utterly dominates its affairs, most especially its hiring and promotion values and actions. As I indicated in Chapter 1, what counts above all is recognition and prestige, objectives that under present arrangements can only be accomplished through visibility and publication.

At schools like Berkeley and UCLA, the usual result is that a professor who does outstanding research will be promoted and retained even if his or her teaching is mediocre or worse. Because teaching has been so enormously undervalued in the research university, a lackluster record in that area is apt to be simply ignored or rationalized by an official evaluation indicating that the professor performs satisfactorily with graduate students or in other "small group settings." The latter judgment, in fact, is frequently a tell-tale sign that the professor is especially ineffective as a teacher, especially with the undergraduates who usually comprise the majority of the student population. The reverse rarely if ever occurs. An exceptional record of teaching, advising, and other internal educational accomplishments without the requisite research record almost inevitably leads to dismissal. Indeed, in my own seventeen years of multiversity experience, I know of no one promoted to tenure on the basis of a distinguished educational record alone. A more common result, in fact, is that such a record evokes considerable peer group suspicion, therefore increasing the likelihood of a negative determination at promotion time.

These realities of academic life are quickly made apparent to newly appointed faculty members. They soon become aware that research in accepted areas and publication in the proper journals are the surest paths to career security. The tight academic marketplace adds additional pressures to young men and women who, like their counterparts in business, law, medicine, and other areas, are eager to do well and are thus inclined to do whatever will pay off and please whomever can advance their status.

Throughout university life, these realities are widely known and often candidly discussed. Recently, I had occasion to discuss these issues with a young professor in a natural science department at UCLA. Known by hundreds of undergraduates as a concerned and effective teacher, he is painfully cognizant that outstanding efforts in this direction will not be advantageous. In a recent meeting with the Chairperson of his Department, he was informed what was required of him in order to pass his upcoming formal review. When I asked him about the balance of teaching and research, he remarked that research would count for about 98% of the review and that teaching about 2%. Most insiders in research universities know that such a comment is hardly facetious.

This young professor has many counterparts throughout the country. I have spoken about this phenomenon with high administrative officials at Berkeley, UCLA, and several comparable institutions. In off-the-record conversations, they are astonishingly candid about the actual operations of promotion policies. Some have, in the privacy of office conversations, indicated that the 50-50 ratio of teaching and research is a sham, designed more for external consumption for regents, state legislators, newspapers, and the public - but not for internal review and tenure committees.

The problem, of course, is that these realities discourage an active involvement in undergraduate education, a phenomenon that is especially tragic in the case of the relatively few professors who are well suited intellectually and emotionally to excel in that domain. For young faculty members in particular, the pressures to publish quickly are intense, for the first formal review occurs within two or three years of appointment. It is therefore essential to have a strong research record, both in print and in progress, to present to one's academic superiors.

It is important to understand some of the specific unfortunate implications of these career pressures. Many new Ph.D.'s, recently hired as Assistant Professors in research universities, do work directly related to their dissertations. Frequently, they exploit their doctoral topics for several years in order to derive as many publication credits as quickly as possible. The result, however, is further immersion in intellectual esoterica. What can happen is that these young professors start to lose sight of the broader relationships of knowledge because of their own sense of urgency to develop expertise in narrow areas of scholarly research. This incentive toward extreme specialization and rapid publication works to the profound disadvantage of undergraduate students, who above all need encouragement to think synthetically and to understand the connections between the various courses in which they are enrolled. Ironically, newly hired faculty are usually assigned to teach introductory courses to freshmen and sophomore students. In these courses particularly, educational sense dictates intellectual breadth and an avoidance of narrow topics suited, at best, to advanced graduate students and fellow professionals. The institutional demand for early faculty publication, however, virtually ensures that the introductory course will be educationally inappropriate.

The research priority of multiversity promotion policies regularly retards the development of young faculty members as effective teachers. The time to test and perfect one's instructional approaches and methods is during the first few years of professorial life. This is the time to experiment, to seek counsel from teachers recognized as exceptional, and especially to become intimately acquainted with the educational needs of one's students. This is the time, indeed, to take advantage of the immense energies and enthusiasm of young adulthood. The insidious temptation, however, is to neglect these duties and professional opportunities in favor of the research obligations that promote career advancement. Students, regrettably, encounter the inevitable manifestations of the real nature of university promotion practices: minimal class preparation, repetition of material found in course texts, lack of commentary on papers and examinations, hurried and even rude treatment during office hours, and the presentation of specialized material having little relevance to the goals of general education.

The reasons are clear. Conscientious educational efforts, including rigorous course organization and extensive contact with students, require enormous expenditures of time and emotional energy. The blunt fact of academic life in the multiversity is that these efforts go largely unrewarded. Young professors who decide to take their teaching as seriously as their research do so at considerable professional risk. Few people in any professional field will work for personal satisfaction alone. As long as traditional academic rewards, including tenure, are largely unavailable for educational contributions, there will be little incentive for improving undergraduate education. Consequently, most faculty members will direct their time priorities towards research and publication. The most tragic effect of all is that young academics are socialized into these values very quickly, setting the tone, all too often, for the remainder of their professional lives.

It is worth noting too that the incentive to rush to publication is equally bad for the creation and discovery of knowledge. When men and women are compelled by powerful career pressures to get rapidly into print, they are unlikely to develop those habits of reflection and contemplation that would better inform their intellectual products. Especially for junior faculty members striving for tenure, there is little incentive to sit back and evaluate their work, to revise their efforts, to learn the context and traditions from which their scholarly production emerges, and to assess the social, political, and ethical implications of their research. At its worst, the real policies of university promotion impel some academics to cut corners and even cheat in their desperation to advance professionally.

Recent dramatic examples of plagiarism and actual fraud in the manipulation and interpretation of research data only underscore the absurdity of university promotion values and practices. The ethical significance of these practices will be treated in the next chapter.

Few senior administrators and tenured professors in the modern university would deny, at least in private, that research production is the major factor in hiring, promotion, and retention practices. What kinds of scholarly efforts command this exalted status? If indeed the research produced by university professors truly accomplished what its proponents claim, perhaps there would be ample justification for a university reward structure that advances this kind of intellectual endeavor even at the expense of teaching effectiveness and broader educational commitment.

It is time to set the record straight in this domain. Despite the existence of some outstanding academic research that has made a powerful contribution to knowledge and the quality of human life, there is an appalling paucity of intellectual creativity and imagination in contemporary American universities. In all areas of academic life, the natural sciences no less than the humanities and social sciences, the majority of published work is routine and pedestrian, and all too often it is even trivial and pedantic. It is revealing to add that more than a few professors will privately admit that much that passes as scholarly research advances personal careers far more than it advances the frontiers of human knowledge.

In my own experiences, I have encountered such candor many times over the years. Recently, for example, I was conversing with a senior colleague of considerable stature and recognition in his field. When I asked him about the value of his research at the beginning of his career, he remarked that its primary relevance was that it brought him tenure.

There is nothing new about the claim that academic knowledge is less valuable than other forms of intellectual expression. Critics from within and outside the university have written extensively about the limitations and exaggerated claims of scholarly research. A modest review of some highlights of this critical tradition contributes to a fuller understanding of the dominant values in the modern research university. More specifically, it fosters a sharper awareness of the particular kinds of research products that receive favor in the promotion and tenure apparatus in virtually all research institutions in contemporary America.

David Bazelon, a provocative American social critic, decided early in life that an academic career would not enable him to pursue his intellectual interests with the vigor and originality he demanded. His desire to maintain a sense of speculative thought and to connect ideas to life could not find expression within the structures of academic research. His comments about this ironic phenomenon are perceptive and revealing: .

> Traditional academic scholarship is no longer an adequate way of conducting man's primary intellectual business. For one thing, the scholarly mode is accumulative, and in no hurry to get back into the flux of life. For another, it assumes that the truly useful books have already been written and need only to be discovered, read, and understood. And it confuses data and quotation collection with important ideas. It is possible to repeat every idea Freud had without having one of your own. Summarizing Freud and making his thought more readily available than he did may well be significant work. But it must not be misunderstood as the most central intellectual work ... Take the characteristic yes-I-read-it-carefully function away from scholarship, and you will have some difficulty defining (and glorifying) what remains.[6]

Bazelon's critique of academic research as merely derivative has been echoed by numerous academics who have grown dissatisfied with the narrowness of the scholarly work that emanates from American research institutions. Walter Kaufmann, the late distinguished philosophy professor at Princeton University, wrote at length on the academic transformation of philosophy. Noting that the great philosophic masterpieces were written by "amateurs," he indicated that the professionalization of the field has made it profoundly unlikely for a Descartes, a Spinoza, a Hobbes, or a Hume to emerge from university ranks. In expressing this with both great clarity and great regret, Kaufmann provides some powerful insights into the structure and values of

77

modern universities and provides a strong clue into the kinds of research efforts that are presently acceptable to most promotion committees: .

> What is new is that philosophy has become a profession - a job rather than a vocation ... The most fundamental change in philosophy is that formerly there were perhaps a dozen men engaged in it at any one time, ... while today there are thousands... [T]housands who have to publish now and then to gain some recognition, to win raises and promotions, and to show themselves and fellow members of their 'association' that they are both physically and mentally alive ...

> What used to be a rare vocation for uncommon individuals who took a bold stand has become an industry involving legions. Naturally, the whole tone and level of discussion has had to change ... The new, professional philosopher does not vie with the great philosophers of former ages ... One publishes papers in learned journals, often employs symbols even when they are dispensable, and uses a jargon that stumps everybody but fellow professionals.

> In philosophy it is respectable to give elaborate accounts of bygone theories in matters it would not be respectable to theorize oneself. To report other men's unsound criticisms is considered worthy ... ; to offer sound criticisms ... on one's own is not considered part of a philosopher's job.

> Clearly, the scholarly monograph is the best way to of making some kinds of contributions; but it would be a pity if the monographic mind monopolized the field.

> Too many [academic] philosophers ... strive for a competence that is always at its best - professional, craftsmanlike, even slick ...[7]

Kaufmann's depressing observations of a quarter century ago have applications far beyond the academic discipline of philosophy. His conclusion that "acceptable" academic research in that field must be competent, narrow, and technical applies equally well to most academic disciplines today. Throughout the university, originality, boldness, and intellectual speculation have been displaced by a far more precise but also a far more limited form of mental expression. The major reason is that the latter efforts lead to tenure and status while the former lead to academic oblivion and probable unemployment.

Perhaps no critic in recent years has been as perceptive about the limited value of university research as Andrew Hacker, professor of political science at Queens College. Writing a little more than a decade ago, his observations constitute a devastating repudiation of the inflated rhetoric in university catalogues about new intellectual discoveries and the stature of professors who ostensibly both transmit and create knowledge:

> Academic knowledge has ceased to be a broad-gauged pursuit of truth and has become instead the accumulation of correct information and interpretations. The lifetime output of a modern scholar can, therefore, consist of quite reputable findings, not a single one of which is liable to attack on the ground that it is in error . . . One only needs to focus on questions where research will yield unexceptionable results, and to eschew topics that might give rise to false reasoning . . . Indeed, the whole concept of "replicable" research assumes that an original mind is neither wanted nor needed . . . Few scholars can afford to stand their ground with the eccentric assertion, "This is the way reality appears to me." Rather, pains are taken to exorcise personality from perception, and the message becomes "This is reality when viewed through the lens of this method." If the methodology is professionally acceptable, . . . then the elements of reality it reveals are usually quite commonplace . . .

Scholarly research has therefore become an esoteric, even occult subcompartment of human knowledge. Contemporary scholarship has become seriously alienated from the reality it purports to examine: it is published separately, discussed in removed surroundings, and defines its focuses in terms of its own choosing . . . .This is why an increasing number of individuals outside the academy have concluded that there is little in current scholarship to augment their intellectual understanding.[8]

Professor Hacker has identified many of the less romantic features of academic research fostered by contemporary university values and preserved through the socialization process of hiring and promotion. The awareness of a few other elements of modern scholarship contributes even further to the view that an awesome gap exists between the ideals and the actualities of university life. It is important to explore these elements in some depth in order to understand why the rhetoric of academic research should be approached with great caution.

Ever since the Soviet Union launched its satellite Sputnik, the status of science has risen dramatically. In the 1950's and 1960's, immense amounts of federal and corporate money poured into research universities in the drive to catch and surpass Russian efforts in space and technology. The effect in universities was to elevate the natural sciences to the top of the academic hierarchy. This in turn generated other, more subtle changes in the university. Foremost among them was the value accorded to various forms of scholarly research. With the ascendancy of science, it became expedient for other fields to try to emulate at least the forms of scientific investigation. In the past few decades, this has meant that quantitative research has come to represent the standard of research excellence and prestige. This is true not only in its natural sphere of biology, chemistry, physics, and astronomy, but also in the social sciences and increasingly in the humanities. The presentation of numbers - the accumulation of data - has come to be valued most highly by promotion committees and thus by the research professoriate throughout the country.

It would be foolish to deny the value of data in the abstract. A great deal of quantitative research combines intellectual rigor and social utility. But it is necessary to examine closely some of the broader and perhaps unintended consequences for other forms of intellectual endeavors that have lost status in the era of numerical domination. Professors whose research work is more qualitative and less subject to empirical verification typically must sustain a higher burden of proof at promotion time. Many must overcome a strong and sometimes unconscious suspicion that their efforts are amateurish and unscholarly. Others are unwilling to take such risks and conform to a value system that approaches a state of national orthodoxy. Attitudes that serve to elevate one small aspect of intellectual work and discourage other approaches with impressive historical roots advance neither the production nor the transmission of human knowledge.

There is an unfortunate and cynical feature of this modern scholarly phenomenon. Many young professors, motivated by visions of rapid advancement and career mobility, have realized that quantitative studies can be generated with astonishing rapidity. All that is required is a set of controllable variables in a suitable experimental setting. With a careful manipulation of these variables, it is possible to produce numerous studies with several sets of quantitative results. These can in turn be published as individual articles in academic journals. Many of these products, not surprisingly, do little to stimulate human thought and even less to serve the educational needs of university undergraduates.

Academic success and reputations are based not only on the kinds of research that professors produce, but also on where they publish their scholarly products. All professors in research universities know that publications in refereed journals and in university presses will count much more highly in promotion and tenure deliberations than efforts published elsewhere. Indeed, in many institutions, only such publications accrue towards promotion, while articles and reports published in "popular" periodicals may actually harm one's chances for tenure. On the surface, this practice appears fairly reasonable, since refereed journals and university presses require peer approval prior to publication. These peers, of course, are fellow professors with demonstrated accomplishments in the specific fields in which manuscripts are submitted for consideration.

This process, however, reinforces the dominant value systems of contemporary university life far more than it fosters widespread intellectual understanding. The mechanism of peer approval for faculty publications is generally effective in screening out the poorest publications. At the same time, it encourages the kinds of competent, derivative, narrow, and unimaginative research described so perceptively by Professors Kaufmann and Hacker. Brilliant but somewhat offbeat or eccentric efforts are as likely to be rejected as poorly reasoned or inaccurate articles, reports, or book-length manuscripts. The system of scholarly publication is a central feature of professional socialization. Little else maintains the academic guild as effectively.

Academic research leading to promotion is thus predominantly conventional and unprovocative. With rare exceptions, it is also heavily laden with jargon and scarcely comprehensible to the intelligent lay public. In fact, its inaccessibility is widely perceived as a virtue. Like doctors, lawyers, and other professionals, academics apparently find it comforting to speak and write in forms of private language that mystify those who exist outside the fraternal order. Unfortunately, this is no harmless professional affectation. An academic profession responsible, among other things, for increasing literacy and promoting verbal clarity should serve as a model of lucid expression. Obscure scholarly articles and books ill serve the student population and the broader society of which it will soon be a leading part.

An equally unfortunate concomitant to the academic promotion process is the disparagement of those relatively few professors who write clearly and communicate their work to non-academic audiences. Scholars who publish their work in publications read by people outside the academy are apt to be viewed by promotional committees as "mere" popularizers, probably the most pejorative (and in career terms, dangerous) appellation in academic life. A curious form of snobbery exists in most research universities, operating on the silly assumption that if many people can read and understand an article or a book, it must somehow be superficial or otherwise intellectually suspect. The educational implications of such an attitude are both negative and obvious.

Beyond all the formal criteria and informal practices that dominate the promotion and tenure operations of university existence, there is one element that is more important than anything else. A professor who "fits in" and who is well liked by those in power is apt to advance professionally, while one who does not fit in and is not liked is apt to be denied promotion. In the most basic way, this is the major determinant of academic advancement, a subjective human factor that far transcends the value of one's actual accomplishments in either teaching or in research. This too is close to a universal feature of organizational life, and it is worth adding that it is not necessarily even conscious.

Professors are like most people in institutional settings. They prefer to work with those with whom they are comfortable, not only in sharing basic attitudes and values, but also in more subtle ways relating to the nuances of personality and ethnic and social class standing. Similarly, they prefer to get rid of those who clash with their personalities and who depart from their complex of social, cultural, and political dispositions. No grand formulation of peer review and academic quality control can repeal this apparently immutable feature of human nature.

Because the realities of promotion and tenure in universities are so profoundly subjective, there is enormous latitude in retaining those who are well liked and releasing those who fall short on this score. There are, to be sure, some limits to such flexibility. The most ingratiating professor who has never published and who has a poor or mediocre teaching record will likely fail in his or her quest for tenure. And the most indecorous Nobel prize winner will surely succeed in a similar quest for academic advancement. But all university insiders know of cases where faculty members of modest intellectual accomplishments manage to make it through the tenure process. It is always possible to rationalize advancement of colleagues of pleasant disposition and middling talent by an official judgment that they have stressed quality over quantity, have revealed considerable promise for future efforts, and have been of extraordinary departmental and campus service. Insiders also know of many cases where the reverse occurs, with a similar pattern of rationalizations in the form of official evaluative prose. Far too many personally unliked scholars with sound academic achievements have failed the promotion hurdle because their work is judged as "beyond the scope of departmental concerns," "insufficiently original," "published in journals of inferior stature," or variants of such negative terminology.

It is worth noting too that in prestigious research universities, promotion and tenure also depend on the judgments of outside reviewers from other universities in the same area of scholarly work. The power to select those to whom promotion files are sent is little short of absolute. In an academic universe in which the attitudes and values of authorities throughout the nation and the world are well known, it is easy to predict the results, pro or con, well in advance of the actual evaluation. This power too enables senior professors to implement their own subjective wishes that depart from the more formal criteria of academic advancement. I should add that, whether consciously or not, this power of external review has often worked to the disadvantage of young female and minority group professors, who are more likely to differ in temperament, values, and academic interests and concerns.

These, then, are some of the realities of university life that are implemented through the process of promotion and tenure. As they stand, they hardly justify the devastating price that must be paid in terms of the massive deemphasis of teaching in particular and education in general. There is an even darker side to this phenomenon, and no critique of contemporary promotion practices would be complete without a glimpse into the human dimensions and social implications of the widespread terminations of outstanding teachers in research universities.

Ever since the activism of the 1960's, critics of modern higher education have claimed that teaching has been fundamentally ignored in faculty personnel decisions. They have also maintained that promotion practices tend to perpetuate both political and academic orthodoxies in an ironic perversion of the classic commitment to academic freedom. Defenders of present university arrangements usually respond by claiming that a more equitable balance in teaching and research has been established in recent years and that the system of institutional checks and balances prevents the imposition of political or other illegitimate criteria in the promotion process.

These competing perceptions are presented regularly and often passionately. Advocates of each position usually rely on anecdotal evidence that they and their friends have seen during their periods of university association. The primary reason for the lack of hard testimentary or documentary evidence lies in the practice of confidentiality that has remained fundamental to the process of appointment, promotion, and tenure review. Consequently, materials are largely unavailable for investigators of this feature of academic life.

Nevertheless, some documentary materials occasionally become available. They shed light on actual promotion operations and are useful in understanding the underlying values that permeate then. The materials that follow come from the University of California at Berkeley, by most accounts one of the premier research institutions in the entire world. In each case, the materials refer to faculty promotion matters decided during the past decade and a half. Each, moreover, involved professors who were widely regarded as excellent teachers among significant numbers of undergraduate students. Finally, in each case, the professor in question was denied promotion and was terminated from university service. It is this latter result that I regard as the "dark" side of promotion and tenure.

The first case involved an Assistant Professor in a large social science department. Highly regarded among undergraduate and graduate students alike, he had repeatedly received rave reviews in student publications that rated the instructional effectiveness of Berkeley faculty members. He had, in addition, produced several reviews, articles, scholarly presentations, and a complete book manuscript on a topic within his field.

The Departmental Review Committee evaluated his record in accordance with the applicable criteria for promotion. The result was an obvious disappointment for the professor and for his students:[9]

Our conclusion is that the present departmental review should be unfavorable. He has achieved an excellent reputation as a teacher and has performed valuable service to the Department, but his scholarship is not of the caliber that would merit promotion, and he shows no promise of improving his scholarship substantially in the near future.

The comments were elaborated in depth in the body of the report. The remarks about his teaching were unambiguous:

From this evidence, student opinion is overwhelmingly enthusiastic about his teaching. The qualities most remarked are his command of his material, his deep interest in his students, and his warm, open relations with them, and his devotion of time and effort beyond that normally expected . . . . His handling of seminars also received high praise . . . [H]e presents a broad scope of reading with which he is thoroughly familiar, encourages free discussion and draws out the newer and more retiring students, resists the temptation to lecture, yet keeps the discussions under control. In his lecture course he provided extra discussion sessions and for graduate students preparing Ph.D. examinations he has run a series of mock orals. He has provided the Department with the text of two lectures . . . and two papers delivered at scholarly meetings . . . these bear out his gift for lecturing with wit and grace, able to impart information while delighting his audience.

The report on the Assistant Professor's scholarship is slightly more extensive. Concluding that his writings reveal both strengths and weaknesses, the Departmental Review Committee reported that he writes with "elegance and grace" and with an impressive knowledge of the literature in his field. At the same time, the Committee concluded that his best work is really "high level popularization" and that a certain lack of intellectual toughness pervades his published and unpublished scholarship. The final paragraph of the review provides a summary of his total accomplishments during his career as a university professor of junior status:

> This committee concludes that [he] is a good teacher, greatly appreciated for his human qualities, that he is a competent and intelligent scholar, but that he is not an outstanding scholar, not a peak performer. Since we see no prospect of change in this judgment, we recommend that his review be unfavorable.

When the report was presented to the entire department, the full tenured staff voted by a substantial margin in favor of the recommendation. In reporting the departmental decision to the Dean of the College of Letters and Science that he should be terminated, the Chairman appended his own remarks and those of two professors who dissented from the majority. Excerpts from each provide a revealing glimpse into the inner workings of the university.

The Chairman reported the consensus of the department as follows:

> The deliberations in this case were lengthy, and the committee reached some definite conclusions . . . The strongest part of his record has been his teaching. He has been remarkably successful in establishing close relations with students and in encouraging them; he is a very popular instructor in the department . . . However, the Tenure Committee did not find evidence of intellectual distinction in [his] scholarship . . . [He] has been a valuable member of our department, and he deserves a merit increase and an opportunity, in these difficult times, to find a suitable academic position. And in view of the University's budget situation, it may not be possible to hire a replacement . . . for several years. We badly need [his] services for the next two years.

An excerpt from one of the dissenters adds to the understanding of the specific case as well as it reveals some of the major conflicts of modern academic existence:

> [His] rare qualities as a teacher and an intellectual being should not be overlooked in any general assessment of the man and his written work to date. He has talents as a teacher that are denied to most of the professors I

have encountered over the years, and he has qualities as a scholar that are only just beginning to come to light . . . In my judgment, his abundant vitality and enthusiasm, his intellectual accomplishments to date, and his commendable avoidance of the safe and narrow subjects which attract men and women of more modest abilities, hold out much promise for the future.

When the file reached the office of the College of Letters and Science, the Dean was obviously disturbed. In forwarding the materials to the Budget Committee, the promotion review unit of the campus, the Dean indicated his personal apprehension about the case:

I must confess that there is enough merit in both [his] teaching and scholarship to give me pause, wondering whether the decision to terminate is wise at this time . . . With the above background in mind, and particularly in view of the unusually good teaching record, I will say that the decision to terminate troubles me.

The Budget Committee was not persuaded and affirmed the departmental recommendation. Its conclusion was for all practical purposes the final word on the case:

The . . . Committee takes note of what the subcommittee calls "an excellent reputation as a teacher and [The] Dean also refers to the teaching record. At the same time we must frankly confess that [his] research seems to be unimpressive . . . We agree with [The] Dean that a terminal appointment can always be reopened if remarkable improvements in the record occur, but for the time being we believe that it is the better part of caution to agree with the tenure staff of the . . . Department to give [him] an increase . . . and *not* to renew his appointment.

At the expiration of his terminal appointment, this faculty member left the university and sought academic employment elsewhere, a task that is always disruptive in human terms and that is compounded by the dismal job prospects in his particular academic discipline.

The second case also involved an Assistant Professor in a large social science department. He too was widely perceived by students as an inspiring and effective teacher, although the record in the latter case is perhaps not quite as strong. In this instance, the case became a matter of considerable campus controversy. Students mobilized against the department's decision to terminate him and the conflict involved allegations of political discrimination as well as more traditional charges that teaching was undervalued in favor of research.

In accordance with university procedures, the promotion case was referred initially to a departmental review committee of senior professors. In a lengthy document that treated every aspect of his academic performance, committee members reached a mixed judgment that recommended a continuation of his status as an untenured junior member of the department. Their report goes into depth in providing the rationale for this recommendation:

> Acting as a Mid-Career Review Committee, the undersigned members of the department have examined [his] academic record and have unanimously come to the conclusion which they submit to the department in the form of the following recommendations:
>
> (1) The Committee concluded that [he] had demonstrated sufficient ability, promise, and diligence in the performance of his duties and recommends that he be reappointed to another term . . .
>
> (2) At the same time the Committee concluded that [he] had yet failed to develop a firm sense of purpose and direction, and felt that an eventual tenure decision in the future will likely depend upon his ability to establish a more well-defined intellectual identity by completing a mature piece of scholarly work and by producing a more focused repertoire of courses that would clearly mark out the nature of his contribution to the teaching program of the department.

The report proceeded to make an assessment of his general and specific contributions and deficiencies:

1. General Assessment
The members of the Committee were in general agreement . . . That [he] possesses a keen intellect and devotion to his academic duties. There was no doubt . . . that in the first two years of his teaching career [he] has successfully accomplished the first stage of development from successful graduate student to independent, creative scholar. At the same time the Committee could not fail to notice [his] recent soul-searching and apparent doubts concerning his own record and the style of work he had been trained to do by his graduate department . . . To state it another way, we were impressed by the seriousness with which he has subjected his previous methods and ideas to unsparing scrutiny. The question is whether this will continue and whether he will be able to arrive at a new, equally productive synthesis between commitment and analytic rigor.

What the report hints at becomes increasingly clear in subsequent documents: trained as a traditional social scientist, this professor had begun to wonder about the estrangement of social science from important aspects of modern social life. He had also begun to develop a major critique of his own discipline and of the broader society of which he was a member. His new academic direction centered around his attempt to create a fusion of intellectual analysis and social action designed to address the ills of contemporary American society.

In judging his publication record, the committee indicated that his record gave promise of future growth in several areas of research. Since this was a mid-career review and not a judgment for tenure, no final determination was required. The report concluded that his potential would "depend on his ability to sort out personal and intellectual experiences and on his capacity to decide where the focus of his scholarly contributions will lie."

The committee also investigated his teaching record in depth:

90

In the less than three years he spent in the department [he] has taught an awesome range of courses in at least four fields . . . and at every level of instruction . . . Moreover, he not only offered this variety of courses but re-prepared them practically each time he was offering them, using considerable boldness in experimenting with new forms . . . [H]e has also taken an important part in the guidance and supervision of advanced work . . . [H]e chaired two guidance committees and participated in five (with two dissertations completed). Currently he is chairman of three dissertation committees while participating in six others.

This impressive teaching record must be analyzed . . . (1) [He] has been a popular and effective teacher with considerable skill in presenting his ideas to diverse audiences, (2) he appears to be particularly effective in lectures. While his undergraduate seminars appeared to inspire many, they also elicited adverse comment as to "lack of structure" and their "excessive freedom". . . . (3) while students would be able to discern intellectual and political bias, [he] has been unanimously praised for his broadmindedness and tolerance for divergent views, and (4) finally, there seemed to be little doubt . . . that he is dedicated, hardworking and that he regards teaching as his true vocation.

This apparently favorable conclusion was qualified by other elements in the teaching record of this professor. What follows illuminates the political context of the case and lends itself to the committee's odd final judgment on his total accomplishments as a university teacher:

Against these constants we will have to weigh some variables. Most significantly, the latter concern the contents of his courses. At first . . . [he] presented a "standard fare" to the students . . . with a sprinkling of "esoteric" materials. [After]wards, however, there has been a rapid change toward the less conventional, with emphasis on a radical critique of [the discipline] and reality, as well as an anecdotal, biographical materials outside formal [social science] . . . This change in intellectual content was accompanied by a change in teaching style, with lectures apparently designed to generate personal involvement and experience, rather than focusing upon the customary intellectual concerns of the profession.

. . . [He] largely discounts prevailing views on the American political system, takes as his premise that the system is beyond redemption, and addresses himself to the question of how to change the social and political order to accomplish a more human "self-actualizing" social context. The one member who read [his lecture notes] carefully found it a potpourri of prevalent radical theories, cliches, and oratory. As such it is often overly emotional, occasionally intemperate, and generally uneven (mixing well-reasoned argument with a somewhat stale and time-worn economic critique of imperialism, capitalism, and liberal democracy). Yet at the same time it also presents an interesting portrait of the intellectual turmoil of our times, and as such it may become a legitimate contribution to our teaching program provided that [he] will show sufficient discipline to test out his ideas, and separate his emotional involvement from the intellectual contents of his presentation . . .

What all this adds up to is that at the present time, it is still impossible to produce a comprehensive evaluation of [him as a] teacher. Given [his] past performance there is no reason to believe that he will not demonstrate the ability to achieve pedagogical maturity and growth, but such growth cannot now be taken for granted.

This report followed standard institutional procedure and was presented to the department Chairman, who in turn submitted the recommendation for a two-year non-terminal renewal to a vote of the senior professors. The recommendation was defeated by a narrow margin; instead, the tenured staff voted that he should be granted only a one-year*terminal* reappointment. The Chairman duly reported this result to the Dean of the College of Letters and Sciences:

> I would like to recommend a merit increase . . . for [him]. In addition, as a result of a meeting of the tenured faculty members of the department, . . . I recommend that [his] appointment be terminated [in one year] . . .

> A large part of the debate turned on the amplitude of the swing of [his] early concern with scientific aspects in the study of social and political life to one now of "an adequate understanding of political action (with its links to freedom and community)" by which [he] hopes to develop a "better comprehension of most of the pressing problems . . . which wrack our country endlessly."

> While those who voted against [him] clearly recognize his ability to do abstract analysis as represented in his initial work, they have serious doubts that he has the talent to successfully and objectively undertake these new concerns. Others . . . clearly felt that he should have the benefit of the doubt; and, [one professor] . . . in particular felt that he was trying to think about [political and social life] in a new manner and that in time he could develop a new synthesis and an intellectual frame of reference which would permit him to do very promising work. This concern over the shifting intellectual interests of [this Assistant Professor] . . . flowed over into criticism regarding his teaching. I would draw your attention to the . . . report in which it states that the lectures are "apparently designed to generate personal involvement and experience rather than focusing upon the customary intellectual concerns of the profession."

> . . . [N]onetheless, in both solicited and unsolicited letters that I have received, [his] teaching tends to be extremely well received by these students, even though they do not necessarily agree with him. That he puts

an enormous amount of effort into his teaching cannot be denied, but the content of some of his courses tends to raise serious doubts as to his maturity . . .

Shortly after sending this letter to the Dean, the Chairman informed the Assistant Professor of the recommendation for termination. His response was to formally request that the tenured staff reconsider their judgment in light of new evidence of scholarly production. The faculty again considered the matter and by a large majority voted not to re-open the case. The Chairman then reported to the Dean that the departmental decision was final.

Meanwhile, the entire file had been forwarded through channels to the Budget Committee. Recognizing the complexity of the case, this committee appeared to oppose the departmental decision to terminate the Assistant Professor in one year. The specific language is revealing, although at least one subsequent document casts possible doubt about the sincerity of the Budget Committee's presentation:

What the . . . committee is worried about are the clearly audible undertones of ideological, if not political, cleavage in the [departmental] staff . . .

Similar problems are visible in the evaluation of [his] teaching . . . The subcommittee has very good things to say about "this impressive teaching record" but . . . there is some criticism with regard to [his] critical posture on the American political system . . . A number of good things are said about his laudable service to the department and about his activities in national professional societies . . .

The Budget Committee is . . . reluctant . . . to accede to [the] request for termination. If we were dealing with a problem of promotion to tenure, the Budget Committee would probably be inclined to interpret a vote which splits the department right down the middle as an indicator for termination as a better course of action. We feel, however, that the ambiguities and ambivalences . . . in the record should recommend some caution, and we would rather recommend that [he] receive a merit increase without a formal notice of termination, and that [the] Chairman [should inform him] about the serious problems raised with regard to his objectivity in scholarship and teaching; . . .

The public character of this case had by then generated considerable interest among high university officials. Among these officials was the Dean of Letters and Science. Writing to an administrative superior, the Dean expressed even more severe misgivings than he had in the first case presented in these documentary accounts:

I may also infer, from considerable knowledge of the Department, that we are witnessing not merely an argument over the quality of a man, but also a struggle of a few against an established orthodoxy . . . To make matters worse, [he] has chosen to bring his side of things conspicuously into the public view, with some exaggeration born of his resentment over his treatment by his colleagues. Equally on the defensive, the majority of his colleagues have solidified in their negative evaluations of his work, which I suspect is not as bad as is claimed. Another point troubles me deeply. In the original presentation, [the] Chairman did not, it now appears, provide me with all of the student opinions on [his] teaching which was then available. In fact, the picture of his teaching given then was neither balanced nor complete. In the present letter from [the] Chairman, he makes brief mention of the fact that he has recently received numerous communications from students on the subject of [the Assistant Professor's] teaching . . .

The fact is that I have read enough letters from students, and have talked at length with enough students (many of whom are well acquainted with me) to know beyond doubt that his teaching contains much intellectual stimulation and substance. To many, his methods may be eccentric, and his politics surely show in his lectures; but I must say frankly that . . . students are safer in the hands of someone

95

who minces no words about his own views, while giving the students the apparatus to develop their own (whether those opinions agree with his or not). The University should probably not be made up only of [people like this man] but it would not be a University without a few of them.

The Dean simultaneously requested a clarification from the department in this matter. Responding, the Chairman indicated that the department was still split, but that a large majority now supported the decision to terminate. Once again, he indicated that the last vote constituted a firm departmental action. The implication was that the majority fully expected support from higher university officials.

The Dean reiterated his own view of the matter. In his letter to presiding campus authorities, he argued strongly that the Assistant Professor's teaching record had been of high quality. Maintaining that a two-year terminal appointment with a possible reconsideration would be more just, he offered several cogent observations about contemporary academic life:

And here we get to the core of it. If one reads the record carefully, he finds that [this professor] came here with all of the best credentials. He was encouraged by his colleagues, and given local and national responsibilities within the fraternity of [social scientists]. Now, suddenly, the weight of opinion has gone against him. Why? . . . Was it that he changed the direction of his research? Frankly I believe that this is the major reason, and for a very profound reason. My experience has been over many years, that the bright young man who chooses new directions . . . is applauded . . . for his imagination and daring . . . and he is given encouragement . . . In this case, [he] receives hostility instead of encouragement, and he receives a terminal appointment . . .

. . . I suggest that we are finding the majority of the members of the Department over-reacting, out of disappointment that their fair-haired boy has forsaken his academic heritage and rejected his ancestors . . .

As I have implied before, I think that the Department needs [him] more than he needs them. I have watched departments closely for long enough to know when orthodoxy has developed to the point of crippling the creative contributions of the University to the evolution of . . . collective intellectual development . . . I suspect that the divisions in the Department . . . are rooted in this problem . . . If we take no risks, we will hardly make much progress along new intellectual lines. A risk such as this one is not likely to jeopardize the University, and the outcome could substantially improve us.

Such a vigorous statement evoked instant administrative concern at the highest levels. In a memo to the chief campus official, a close subordinate detailed some of the points in controversy. Responding specifically to the Dean's letter written the previous day, this subordinate revealed either that the earlier formal report of the Budget Committee might have been at variance with the actual views of the members or that he himself had misinterpreted their position:

[A] I don't see his argument . . . at all that [the Assistant Professor] is a brilliant young man who has changed direction. He may be a brilliant young man, but his switch is emotional, not intellectual.
[B] I think we have two problems here: [the Assistant Professor] and [the] Dean (more in a heat about this one that I can remember ever before).
[C] The Budget Committee's recommendation for two years termination was only palliatory and, intentionally, de-fusing student-wise. No doubt there about their guess for the long-run. It is negative for [his] future.
[D] I can see the Promotion Review Committee's position; not [the] Dean's; and am uncertain . . . about that of the Department.
[E] I'd suggest that we cut the Gordian knot and get it over with: terminal year: [next year]. I think we should back the Department here.

97

Despite this view, the Budget Committee, at least formally, retained its original posture. In two communications to the senior administrator who authored the previous memo, the Committee reommended a two-year term with the possibility of reconsideration. The second communication makes the point clearly even while disclosing broader clues into their own ultimate values:

> The Budget Committee sticks with its original view that [he] should have a two-year appointment in order to give him an opportunity to demonstrate a return to scholarly ways, a return for which we still hold some hope.

This letter was to have no effect whatever. In a directive from the senior official to the Dean dated the previous day, notice was given that the appraisal of the Assistant Professor had been reconsidered and that the outcome was negative, resulting in the one-year terminal appointment originally recommended by the department. Approximately one year later, he was separated from university service. He too had to face the burdens of the academic marketplace, a problem intensified by the formal judgment of the University of California that he was of inadequate academic stature to remain a member of that faculty.

The third case also involved an untenured professor who taught in a European language department. Like the previous cases, this involved a man who was widely respected by students for his vigorous and inspiring teaching and for his willingness to treat controversial topics avoided by his departmental colleagues. In this case, he was known as an enthusiastic supporter of third world literature written in the colonial European language. His advocacy of this literature as a legitimate supplement to standard European literature was the source of severe, even bitter divisions within the department. Unlike the second case, the matter never occasioned widespread campus or public controversy. The documents reveal, however, that the case raised grave doubts about the administrative operations of the department. In time, these doubts were sufficient to impose a series of traumatic departmental changes.

As usual, the conflict was triggered by a departmental decision to terminate the professor. Because neither the departmental review nor the Chairman's letter is available, the first relevant document is the evaluation of the Budget Committee. Responding to a substantial majority vote to terminate, the Committee in unusually sharp language called attention to a series of blatant irregularities and academic improprieties, conduct which was later proved to influence even its own judgment:

> This department is notorious for bad personnel management and for extraordinarily long letters of personal attack . . . the Budget Committee shares [the] Dean's distaste for these hatchet jobs, and observes that some of the blows are badly aimed.

Having expressed its own repugnance for the intemperate tone of official departmental reports on this professor, the Committee proceeded to draw its own conclusions on the basis of the usual promotion criteria. In the area of research, the judgment was that the record was inadequate and that his involvement with Third-World literature had been unimpressive in terms of translations and articles.
The evaluation of his teaching, however, was slightly more favorable:

> This is [his] strong point, and presents the classic spectacle of an enthusiastic, vigorous instructor careless of academic tradition and prone to experiment, whose activities are resented by his colleagues for catering to the students' basest whims, etc. The Budget Committee believes that many of the strictures expressed in [the Chairman's] letter are unjustified and unfair. Nonetheless, an examination of the copious material submitted by [the man] himself suggests that the "uncritical" spirit of which his colleagues complain is indeed a feature of his teaching . . . The Budget Committee would not be surprised to learn that (though we have not been told) [he] has an enthusiastic following among students to whom he has made . . . literature--or at least, [Third-World] literature--relevant. The evidence suggests, however,

99

that this desirable conclusion is reached only by way of simplification and superficiality.

In a note appended to the report, the Committee continued its assault on the departmental leadership:

> Sensible review of [this] case was frustrated . . . by the evasive incompetence of [the] former Chairman . . . It has been hindered . . . by the obsessive, seemingly vengeful "overkill" of [the present] Chairman.

The Committee's decision to concur in the termination was not to be a final judgment. The Assistant Professor had complained vigorously that he had been unfairly treated in his promotion case. The Dean agreed and indicated that a new review should be established. This was done by the department and within a few weeks he was notified of another negative decision. Meanwhile, the central administration was conducting an investigation into the operations of the department. A special review committee concluded that irregularities had occurred on a widespread basis. The result was a change in the departmental leadership. The new Chairman ordered a re-evaluation of all pending promotion cases.

In due course, the senior professors in the department again convened to consider the promotion file. Consisting of the same persons who had twice earlier voted for termination, the third vote was hardly surprising. Although the new Chairman had assured the Assistant Professor that this time an impartial review would be conducted, the Assistant Professor replied that the earlier improprieties would fatally color his chances for genuinely fair treatment. He underscored his protest by arguing that colleagues who had sought his termination with evident passion could hardly be expected to transcend their prejudices by administrative fiat.

In reporting the new termination vote to the Dean, the Chairman appended a lengthy document that treated the complexities of the case in depth. Unhappy about the outcome, he nevertheless declined to contest the final departmental verdict. In his report, he disclosed that the review of the professor's research was negative, although clearly different from the overwhelmingly critical reports of earlier recommendations. His book on a major European author was judged "simply not a distinguished piece of work," although favorable comments were also made part of the record. The record also indicates that some scholars from other universities had a much higher view of the book. One authority, for example, wrote that "his book will be a signal contribution . . ." He also wrote that "it is lively, perceptive, and intelligent."

The Chairman's comments on the professor's teaching is the most important feature of his report and provides a new perspective on the earlier conclusions of the Budget Committee:

> Finally, there remains the matter of his teaching: here I think it is important to enter a correction into the record. The previous Chairman's letter[s] . . . contain a number of extremely damning paragraphs on [his] pedagogical performance. [He] is accused of propaganda, of indoctrination, and of demagogy; of making of his own course a preachment in inverted racism; of gaining easy popularity through glibness; of making his courses distorted and unbalanced sermons on political issues; of perverting his subject; of spuriousness, superficiality, eccentricity, meretriciousness, and a "wholly uncritical attitude" toward his materials. For all these extraordinary assertions, hardly a shred of evidence is offered . . . There is no attempt to ask whether such picturesque pedagogy might not also have been intellectually responsible and academically valid; instead it is assumed throughout that his popularity was achieved by ignoble means. His teaching is roundly declared to be . . . a rather arrogant disregard of accepted academic restraints. No evidence is offered for this devastating ascription . . . In short, . . . the most crushing conclusions were arrived at on the basis of rank hearsay, by a group of scholars who would be aghast at the thought of reviewing a book without first reading it, not to speak of clobbering it to death because of their personal dislike for the author.

In my view, our meeting . . . produced a clear reversal of this judgment, and a vindication of [his] teaching. [One professor], charged with the report on . . . teaching, reached a strongly affirmative verdict . . . He found . . . that . . . his courses followed conventional lines, were highly organized, and involved carefully prepared lectures . . . Finally, the student evaluations: these . . . bore striking witness to [his] pedagogical talents. Without exception, they praised the course as a rich and exciting experience. Students felt that they had learned much about many new things, not only about [the specific] literature, but about literature as an institution, and its relation to their own lives and their own problems. Everything suggests that they felt challenged by the course, that it was an important intellectual event in their lives, and not the cheap exercise in platform demagogy which was thought to be [his] stock in trade.

. . . I myself regard the previous injurious verdict as unequivocally reversed; he has now been shown to be a teacher of exceptional quality.

With the record at least privately corrected as to his teaching, this professor too was terminated and he obtained a teaching position elsewhere. Like the others, however, he had to endure the emotional agonies of an admittedly unfair review and suffer the burdens of an unfavorable tenure evaluation.

These documentary excerpts speak effectively for themselves. A brief summary of their major implications, however, can facilitate a more basic understanding of university faculty personnel practices and the essential values and priorities underlying the modern research institution. This understanding is particularly valuable to students and to the general public, who are thoroughly excluded from the decision-making operations revealed so strikingly in these materials.

A threshold question is whether the three cases are indicative of university conduct in general. In short, there is no easy answer. Only a systematic review of all confidential promotion documents in a given university could furnish a truly accurate picture. Nevertheless, the cases of the three dismissed Assistant Professors are valuable and suggestive for many reasons. I should add that my examination of comparable sets of documents from similar research universities reveals that there seems to be no paucity of similarly questionable policies and practices.

More important, these materials establish some minimal empirical support for the contemporary critics of the modern research university. This support supplements the more speculative charges that teaching is severely undervalued and that a pall of academic and political orthodoxy hangs over much of current life in research universities.

Even if these specific cases are viewed as aberrations, their very existence raises troublesome questions about university operations. In all three cases, dubious practices and policies were confirmed throughout the entire promotion review process. Even though the system was adequate in identifying some of the problems, the final result was entirely unambiguous: each man, despite significant, officially recognized intellectual accomplishments, was in effect fired. Students were denied valued educational services while the individual professors were forced to endure a variety of disruptive personal consequences.

An obvious conclusion emerging from these materials is that university personnel and promotion practices afford no special claim to superior conduct in this realm. Like all professional groups, academics are fond of promoting a heightened image for public consumption. Professors like to proclaim that review procedures are eminently fair, conducted by scholars for whom truth and objectivity are supreme values. The implication is that the evaluation of a professional colleague is as objective and detached as the other functions that form the substance of scholarly life.

The three cases, however, suggest that academic promotion decisions are hardly free of personal biases, resentments, and arbitrary actions. Such conduct originates in the inevitable personality conflicts of human beings. These are universal features of employment relationships. Elevated notions of "peer review" cannot conceal the fact that all personnel actions are influenced by powerful subjective factors. No valuable purpose is served by continued mystification of these matters. Instead, a candid recognition of the human context of academic promotion and tenure would serve to reduce the influence of at least the worst personal prejudices in matters of faculty evaluation and review.

The documentary materials also raise disconcerting questions about the value of teaching in university priority schemes; they provide concrete support for the arguments presented earlier in this chapter. All three of these terminated professors were excellent teachers who clearly had an enormous impact on scores of their students. Official university evaluations confirmed this view for all three men. Significantly, while doubts were presented as to the value of their research accomplishments, all were officially perceived to be at least competent scholars by their peers.

The clear implication is that teaching is not given equal weight in the actual determination, regardless of the official requirement for judgmental parity. The record reveals that no matter how distinguished the teaching, the research record is ultimately determinative in matters of promotion or termination. The young natural science professor at UCLA, about whom I wrote earlier, would, upon seeing these materials, be extremely justified in his apprehension that his outstanding teaching record will do him little good in his upcoming evaluation. A close examination of these documentary excerpts, furthermore, reinforces suspicions that popularity among undergraduate students can generate resentments among less inspiring and creative colleagues. The deplorable result is that uniquely talented people with sensitive gifts for imparting knowledge and stimulating thought have been removed from university service.

This result provokes concern about the professed requirement that excellence in every area of academic life is a condition for promotion. An increasingly complex society requires an increasingly complex division of labor. To require outstanding performance in every realm elevates the probability of either mediocre achievements in all areas or informal neglect of a major function like teaching. Few men and women are so extraordinary that they can do everything spectacularly well. Since few research universities have a surplus of truly exceptional teachers, it seems a dubious policy to fire those fortunate enough to be in that category.

An equally distasteful revelation is the apparent existence of a guild mentality in the multiversity. Especially in the second and third cases, a basic challenge to existing political and academic values evoked considerable hostility in return - emotions that fundamentally colored the entire tenure review process. The themes and methods of the second assistant professor, for example, were highly unorthodox by contemporary standards. He sought both to criticize his own social science discipline and the character of political life in modern America. His view that only radical change could redeem the quality of American life may not be popular among some senior university professors, but it is an arguable and intellectually defensible position. So too is his view that contemporary social science is severely alienated from major features of social and political life.

His insistence that teaching should engage both the cognitive and affective dimensions is similarly a respectable if dissenting view of educational theory and practice. His honest presentation of personal views into the classroom has had ample justification throughout history. The conclusion is inescapable that his unpopular views and teaching practices clouded and ultimately destroyed his chances for promotion. More broadly, this case lends some credence to the suspicion that charges of immaturity and emotionalism may often mask a contemptuous academic attitude toward a breach of political orthodoxy.

The assistant professor in the third case also encountered an entrenched academic position through his insistence that third world literature was a valid academic pursuit. His refusal to accept the more traditional elitist view made him an academic pariah. The real problem is that any elements of orthodoxy should be present at all in an institution purportedly devoted to higher learning. More insidious, of course, is when it is permitted to influence decisions about promotion and tenure. The raison d'etre of a university is to encourage intellectual growth and a wide diversity of ideas. It is appropriate to quote once again from the Dean who so vigorously opposed the termination of the second assistant professor:

If we take no risks, we will hardly make much progress along new intellectual lines. A risk such as this is not likely to jeopardize the University and the outcome could substantially improve us.

There is nothing new in discovering significant gaps between professed policies and actual practices. Such gaps exist throughout social institutions, and universities no less than other organizations are populated by people who are often petty, vain, and defensive. Universities, however, both purport to be, and should be, different from other organizations and institutions. The mandate to create and transmit knowledge sets it fundamentally apart from most government agencies and industrial enterprises. The excessive preoccupation with confidentiality, however, only serves to reinforce these traits and generates grave doubts about the integrity of the entire system of promotions and rewards in the modern university. Candor and openness in this domain would both improve the process itself and help to make the university more accountable to both its students and to the public.

As I noted at the outset of the chapter, the major problem is not whether tenure should be retained or not. Far more basic is whether the system of promotions itself, including lifetime employment security or not, can be adequately reformed so that it truly incorporates reasonable judgments about the actual contributions and merits of university faculty members. Above all, the process must take educational excellence into account; equally important, it must not be abused by reinforcing an anti-intellectual and anti-educational guild mentality. Whether that is really possible in light of the present organizational scheme of university life and in light of the character and personalities of academic men and women is, at best, highly problematic. But the resolution of this question has enormous consequences for millions of people in America and throughout the world.

NOTES

1. There are extremely few exceptions. Only a handful of schools have eliminated tenure and have substituted for it a series of long-term contracts. Two interesting examples are

Evergreen State College in Olympia, Washington and Hampshire College in Amherst, Massachusetts.

2. This chapter will not directly address the issue of the value of tenure. Rather, its focus will be on the effects of promotion and tenure on institutional priorities, especially undergraduate education.
For an interesting critical view of tenure, written by a political conservative, see Robert Nisbet, "The Permanent Professors," in Charles Anderson and John Murray, *The Professors* (Cambridge, Massachusetts: Schenkman, 1971), pp.105-121.

3. Nisbet, op. cit., p.107.

4. By "regular," I mean those men and women holding tenure-track positions, usually Assistant Profesors. Increasingly, universities are relying on more marginal, less expensive academic personnel for much of their instructional operations. These latter people, no matter how accomplished, can not get promoted. The ethical implications of this state of affairs are explored in Chapter 5.

5. Ironically, these senior faculty impose standards that they themselves were never required to meet when they were reviewed for promotion. This is naturally a source of both anxiety and bitterness throughout the university.

6. David Bazelon, *Nothing But a Fine Tooth Comb* (New York: Simon and Schuster, 1969), p.39.

7. Walter Kaufmann, *The Faith of a Heretic* (New York: Doubleday, 1961), pp.60-76.

8. Andrew Hacker, *The End of the American Era* (New York: Atheneum, 1970), pp.199-206.

9. For reasons of personal privacy, I have deleted the specific names of the parties involved. These deletions in no material way alter the substance of these documentary materials nor detract from a broader consideration of their implications.

CHAPTER 5

Corruption and Decay in the Academy: Ethical Abuses in Academic Life

Ethics is big business today in American higher education. Both the undergraduate and the graduate curriculum in most large universities have a dazzling array of offerings dealing with ethical problems in modern life. This is a comparatively recent educational development; only a few years ago, there would typically be two or three courses in ethics in the department of philosophy and perhaps a course or two in the schools of law and medicine. For undergraduates, more often than not, ethics was taught as a discrete subject, divorced from the realities of daily life. Students who enrolled in these courses usually found the same intellectual narrowness and fragmentation they encountered throughout their undergraduate careers.

For more than a decade, however, there has been an increasing public concern about ethics and values, especially as they relate to various features of professional life. There has been a proliferation of articles, debates, and forums among lawyers, doctors, managers, engineers, journalists, and others about their ethical defects, obligations, and responsibilities. There have also been numerous media presentations on this topic geared to more popular audiences in the United States.

There are several reasons why this new focus on ethics and values has developed. In part, it is a legacy of the consciousness and activism of the 1960's. The recent disclosure, moreover, of some glaring professional improprieties has been instrumental in raising issues that professionals have generally sought to avoid. The Watergate scandal was a major crisis for the legal profession because an embarrassingly large number of convicted persons in that affair had been members of the bar. Watergate generated scores of bar association ethics inquiries, law school professional responsibility courses, and a veritable barrage of articles, reports, and proposals for reform. Lawyers and the public, quite properly, wanted to know how people trained in the law could adapt their talents and energies so easily to such illegal and unethical activities.

The medical world has had some similar problems. Fourteen years ago, for example, the infamous Tuskegee experiment of 1932-1972 was exposed, in which doctors from the U.S. Public Health Service observed four hundred black men suffering from syphillis without providing treatment. This grisly affair, uncomfortably similar to the Nazi "medical" experiments, facilitated the creation of human subject protection committees as well as numerous courses and programs in medical ethics.

There are many other reasons for this increased interest in ethical and value questions. In medicine, dramatic technological advances have created complex, ambiguous, and fascinating ethical dilemmas. Organ transplants, intrauterine diagnoses, infant life support systems, and many other developments have caused thousands of people within and outside the medical community to deal seriously with ethical problems that did not exist a generation ago. Technology has also created new and troubling ethical problems in other areas. Computer advances alone have generated issues that scarcely existed in the 1960's and 1970's. Sophisticated information retrieval systems, for example, have caused a serious re-examination of the right to privacy. These systems enable governmental agencies and businesses to rapidly discover intimate details about people's lives. Whether the police should have access to persons' total biographies when they are stopped for minor traffic violations and whether department stores should have the right to know about people's financial dealings twenty years prior to their credit applications are controversial problems. People throughout society will have to grapple with these dilemmas for decades to come.

American universities have begun to deal seriously with these issues of ethics and social policy. Beyond the obvious (and valuable) curricular changes and additions, some universities have established entire programs to deal more systematically with ethical problems and dilemmas throughout social, political, and economic life. In their attempts to explore such problems, some universities have responded impressively if uncharacteristically to a legitimate public

110

concern. Some of the research and public service programs emerging from this university interest in contemporary ethics have been extremely good, a much better reflection of the real potential of academic life.

There is, to be sure, a strong self-interest implicit in this intellectual enterprise. Modern ethical problems have served as excellent avenues of research for professors seeking promotion and career security. Medical, legal, and business ethics have therefore seen a significant proliferation of academic publications in recent years, some of which is sound and perceptive and some of which is dull and pedantic. More important, many universities have entered this area of contemporary social ethics in response to a new vocationally and professionally oriented student population. A curricular treatment of ethics and values has been useful in directing students' understandable occupational interests into more fundamental liberal arts concerns. Indeed, recent experience suggests that undergraduates are highly motivated by the examination of the ethical dimensions of technology and professional life and practice. Institutionally, such courses often draw considerable enrollment, desperately needed for the yearly statistical presentations in support of academic budget requests. Self-interest notwithstanding, this feature of contemporary university affairs is clearly desirable.

University professors have a long history, in fact, of examining and judging the ethical conduct of people in virtually every realm of human endeavor. Ironically, however, the intellectual acuity applied elsewhere is seldom applied to their own institutions and to their own affairs. The modern research university is a complex institution, beset with immense problems as I have sought to describe throughout this book. Because of its values, its organizational structure, and the character of its dominant personnel, it generates vast numbers of ethical problems, most of which are not perceived as such by insiders and are not widely known by the public. Academics are reluctant to acknowledge the existence of serious ethical problems among the modern professoriate. The same loathing to compare themselves with doctors, lawyers, businessmen, and other upper middle class groups is equally applicable here.

There are, however, significant abuses in the world of higher education, and only a naive fool or a cynical apologist would deny the existence of major problems in professional conduct in university settings. The present national interest in broader issues of ethics and values makes it a propitious time to identify the troublesome areas of moral laxity and academic misconduct and to evaluate more closely the proper responsibilities of the academic calling. It is natural that professors and university administrators do not perceive this as a favorite topic of discourse and conversation. They are as sensitive as other professionals in their desire to protect their public and self-images. That understandable impulse, however, tends to discourage a serious treatment of the central ethical defects of their profession.

Such a treatment is vitally necessary today. Any institution with glaring ethical defects will have trouble in fulfilling its primary objectives. The persistence of various forms of academic misconduct defeats the educational aims of the university. Throughout this chapter, I shall show how the entire environment of university life is affected by the existence of problems of professional ethics. This environment places yet another powerful damper on undergraduate education within the setting of the large research institution.

The low priority of undergraduate teaching sets the context for a large complex of irresponsible and unethical practices. Foremost among them is the practice of doing little or no preparation for classroom instruction. All university students have seen instructors who display an indifferent attitude toward the organization of their courses. With little idea of and concern for the thematic and conceptual direction of their classes, many professors come unprepared into class and spend enormous amounts of time rambling - to the usual dismay of their student audiences. Such classes are usually full of repetitious remarks, inadequately developed frameworks for analysis, and minimal attempts to connect course content to broader intellectual ideas and currents. Often they are simply boring, providing little motivation to students to make maximum use of their own capacities for thought and creativity. In large universities, especially in high enrollment introductory courses, organizational efforts are regularly delegated to teaching assistants, with inevitably fortuitous results.

As I have indicated in previous chapters, powerful career and emotional incentives cause university professors to focus their energies on the kinds of research publications that will find favor among traditional academic colleagues. Thus it is understandable that the classroom will suffer neglect. What is understandable, however, is not necessarily justifiable. Very few academics would view this pattern as a major issue of ethics and responsibility; rather, they rationalize it as part of the realities of modern life in research oriented institutions.

It is time to focus more precisely on this problem and to understand it centrally as an ethical issue. Regardless of career pressures, university professors are required to spend much of their efforts and energies in instructional activities. Their university salaries reflect these responsibilities and only a minuscule percentage of university faculty members are presently relieved of all teaching obligations. Theoretically, fully one-half their efforts, even in the most prestigious institutions, are supposed to be directed to their roles as teachers.

No professional activity exists in a vacuum. *Every* feature of professional life, from the most complex to the most mundane, imposes a high level of responsibility on its practitioners. This applies to every field of human endeavor. It includes university teaching as much as legal, medical, psychotherapeutic, and dental practice; certified public accounting; the gathering and interpretation of news; the publication of newspapers, magazines and books; personnel management; and literally hundreds of other professional enterprises. All such activities require the highest levels of competence and commitment. Professional conduct falling short of this standard is negligence. Gross negligence, in turn, is both unprofessional and unethical.

To perceive the defects of undergraduate education without considering ethics both devalues the field of ethics and debases the professional standing of university teaching. There is little difference between a lawyer who fails to prepare adequately for a trial or a deposition, a dentist who is cavalier in performing a routine hygienic procedure, a reporter who neglects to verify the facts of a story, and a university teacher who decides to "wing it" for an hour in class. In each case, unprofessional conduct is present, and no excuses about competing professional pressures and obligations can conceal the ethical laxity that has worked an injustice on the respective professional constituencies.

Within the framework of professional ethical responsibility, it is useful to examine a variety of other defects in the general area of teaching and advising. At the outset, however, an important distinction should be noted. University teachers who plan their courses conscientiously and who make a determined effort to perform their instructional functions well, but who do not succeed, are not guilty of unethical behavior. While their competence may legitimately be questioned, the relevant factors in academic ethical analysis involve most fundamentally the motivations underlying the action or conduct at issue.

A frequent and well justified student complaint is that many professors merely repeat what is written in course texts, thereby reducing substantially the intellectual potential of classroom teaching. This is not a minor matter; the classroom is the environment in which ideas can be developed, implications identified and explored, and connections made to other fields of knowledge and to life in general. It provides the opportunity to explain, to qualify, to debate, and to provide students with opportunities to ask questions, raise objections, and to take a more active role in their own educational lives. Mere repetition of text material profoundly misses the educational point. When done intentionally because it is easier than the intellectually demanding alternative, it is an example of professional negligence that exacerbates the educational deficiencies of the large research university.

Another significant abuse in the instructional realm occurs when professors are habitually absent from their classes and offices. In an academic world characterized by mobility and entrepreneurship, this problem has become acute in recent years. Students have properly complained that they are treated cavalierly by professors who are regularly off to conferences, to research sites, to consulting obligations, or to any other external activity removing them from direct institutional contact with undergraduates. As a result, they are deprived of some of the educational services and benefits to which they are legitimately entitled. A faculty member who notifies students that he or she will be in class or in the office at designated hours has a professional obligation to be faithful to that promise. It is no secret that a notable gap exists between promise and performance.

No one could find ethical fault in a professor who must occasionally be absent from class or office hours because of the ordinary schedule conflicts of life in a complex society. This is inevitable and students are generally sympathetic and tolerant in such circumstances. The ethical problem lies in the habitual character of the omissions and, equally important, the attitudes that underlie such actions. The notion that an office hour is dispensable because it only involves students is simply not an acceptable standard of professional conduct in the university. Of comparable status is the all too common practice of being absent from office hours in substance though not in physical fact. Over the years, several hundreds of students have reported to me how professors have opened mail, held lengthy telephone conversations, or shuffled through papers while ostensibly engaged in personal conversations with students. Serious education must go beyond books, papers, and examinations. It requires regular and close contact with people, especially the faculty in institutions of higher learning. Professors who in attitude and action debase this principle both defeat the purposes of education and abuse the standards of professional responsibility.

This low regard for teaching is further manifested in careless or even non-existent advising. This problem is endemic in the contemporary research university. For professors who perceive their mission to be the advancement of knowledge, long hours in personal advising sessions usually seem dull and ungratifying. Moreover, for the reasons made apparent in Chapter 4, there is little or no reward for conscientious services in this area. In several institutions, the faculty has simply abandoned the advising role altogether. At UCLA, for example, the vast majority of professors do no advising at all. Instead, the function has been delegated to a paraprofessional class of advisors, some of whom are very good and some of whom are not. The same system exists at many other large research universities.

No matter how good non-academic advisors may be, they rarely have the academic background and intellectual perspectives of faculty members. Effective advising must go far beyond a mechanical repetition of course, major, and graduation requirements. It involves a careful integration of personal needs, academic options, and future career or professional plans. Good advising requires careful thought and the ability to communicate sensitively with students of diverse personalities, abilities, and backgrounds. It is as important as any other feature of higher education, and it is especially necessary in large schools with thousands of students. Indifferent attitudes towards advising and the actual abandonment of this role should also be viewed as breaches of educational responsibilities and professional ethics. When done individually, culpability lies with the specific faculty members. When done institutionally, there still exists an ethical problem involving complicity with a policy that denies students the best possible educational services. In both cases, students represent a professional constituency that has received services of lesser caliber and quality than could be provided if the appropriate will were truly present.

Evaluation of student work also lends itself to a pattern of faculty laziness. During my academic career, I have seen literally thousands of student papers to which little or no teacher commentary was appended. Instead, only final grades were present, with no rationale or specific indication of how the efforts might have been improved. In my experience, students are in general deeply disturbed when they receive a grade and nothing else - regardless of whether the grade is superior or not.

This too is no trivial matter. Admittedly, it takes enormous time to read student papers carefully and critically. A short eight or ten page paper can easily take an hour to grade if the professor is duly conscientious and willing to comment extensively on matters of substance and style. A lengthy undergraduate term paper can consume two hours or more. Part of this work can be intellectually engaging, but candor compels an admission that much of it can be tedious and boring, especially in an era of marginal student literacy. And of course no institutional incentive exists to take this function seriously, since no academic review committee is likely to make such efforts a major variable in promotion and tenure proceedings.

Nevertheless, students who put conscientious effort into their written work are entitled to equally conscientious evaluations. This too is a significant part of the educational operations of a university and thus a fully integral feature of the professional obligations of faculty members. Anything short of this standard diminishes the prospects for learning and student improvement. Indeed, when professors are guilty of neglect in this area, it also diminishes the respect of students for the entire educational process. Faculty members who complain about student passivity and lack of intellectual curiosity ought to look to those ethically dubious teaching practices that ironically help to foster such student attitudes.

The overwhelming research priority of modern university life also generates widespread examples of questionable professional conduct. Although still relatively rare in American academic life, plagiarism and falsification of research data are clearly on the rise. Men and women who are desperate - not only to achieve promotion to tenure but also to achieve recognition, visibility, and professional reputations - are sometimes inclined to take short-cuts in their rush to publication. The recent, dramatic case of Harvard medical researcher Dr. John Darsee is an extreme example of what the pressures and priorities of academic life can generate. Over a two year period or more, he produced fraudulent research that, when finally discovered, caused the retraction of seventeen papers and forty seven abstracts. Furthermore, Dr. Darsee's unethical conduct ruined a major research project and caused enormous embarrassment to several leading academic institutions as well as to many prominent scientists.[1] More important, at least fifteen cases of academic fraud have been discovered during the last decade, including young and promising researchers at such prestigious institutions as Yale, Boston University, Sloan-Kettering, Mt. Sinai, and Cornell.[2] Presumably, scores or more of undetected cases of outright fraud and manufactured data exist throughout American higher education, an inevitable consequence of existing pressures and values in the research university.

No one questions the use of the terms "unethical" or "unprofessional" to characterize the conduct of Dr. Darsee and others who cheat in their quests for scholarly recognition. The more subtle problems that recur more frequently in academic life are viewed with greater ambivalence. The seemingly ambiguous practices that invariably accompany the drive for visibility should also, however, be examined for their ethical content and for their implications for broader standards of professional responsibility.

How are these more subtle problems manifested in modern academic practice? Reputation, despite the routine denials of some leading academic administrators, is measured largely by productivity. In essence, quantity becomes the operative standard for scholarly success. Young, aggressive professors and post-doctoral researchers know well that it behooves them to augment their bibliographies as rapidly as possible. In his article on the Darsee case, George Colt described the phenomenon well:

> Fifty publications were once considered a lifetime's work; today, a hundred credits for a researcher in his early thirties is not unheard of. To beef up bibliographies, researchers may slice findings into L.P.U.'s - least publishable units - and get five or six publications for the work of one. Although it's difficult to get printed in the prestige journals (the New England Journal of Medicine accepts twelve to thirteen percent of unsolicited manuscripts), it's simple to get published somewhere; the National Library of Medicine subscribes to 23,000 serial publications.[3]

There are other ways for professors to add publications that work effectively on behalf of careers if only marginally (if at all) for the advancement of human knowledge. Some professors, in essence, publish the same work under a variety of different titles in different journals. Frequently, the research data are altered slightly as a result of some inconsequential change in analysis or interpretation. Sometimes, the changes are largely cosmetic and editorial. Often, the ideas presented have been presented many times before. All university insiders can point to colleagues who have mined the same fields for years or even entire careers. A few years ago, when I served in the National Endowment for the Humanities, I had occasion to see this fraudulent phenomenon in abundance. Because I was privy to literally hundreds of academic resumes, often containing lists of fifty, seventy five, or one hundred or more publications, I wondered how these professors could be so extraordinarily productive. When I spot-checked some of these resumes, I discovered with astonishing regularity that the practice of placing old wine in new bottles was omnipresent indeed.

Publication puffery, I found, existed most strikingly in lists of books purportedly published by many professors. On further scrutiny, I saw that many of the volumes listed as books were really merely edited volumes of articles and reports written by others. Frequently, the only contribution from the editor consisted of a modest or even perfunctory preface or introduction. There is nothing wrong with editing collections of readings; many such publications are useful to scholars and educators. The misconduct occurs when this particular form of intellectual accomplishment is misleadingly presented as something that it is not. This form of deception, regrettably, is far from uncommon.

The most widespread abuses occur in the allocation of authorship in academic articles and papers. Who should properly receive publication credit is sometimes a difficult question. Guidelines are vague and criteria vary from institution to institution and academic discipline to academic discipline. This morally ambiguous context, which will be explored more fully below, should not obscure the misconduct that does occur in American universities.

It is widely known (if not widely discussed), for example, that some faculty members take credit for the work of junior colleagues and graduate students. The feudal character of so much of university life makes this reprehensible practice almost inevitable. Apprentice academic personnel are among the most insecure and vulnerable workers in American society. Dependent upon senior professors for recommendations, contacts, and positive evaluations, they are virtually powerless to stop those who cynically appropriate their scholarly products. I have spoken frequently to young faculty members and even more frequently to graduate students who have been victims of this form of intellectual theft and brutality. Recently, for example, a young instructor at UCLA told me of her experiences as a graduate student at a major research university. For two years, she was employed as a "research assistant" to a well known literary scholar there. During that time, she prepared several "reports" on various topics in his area of scholarly expertise. These reports were later published

119

virtually verbatim, under his name without acknowledgment or attribution to her.

In private, many of the men and women whose work is stolen and inadequately acknowledged complain bitterly about this practice. At the same time, however, they bemoan the fact that the system provides little or no remedy for their plight. That it does not should be (but in general is not) a central concern of all personnel in modern universities, but especially senior faculty members and academic administrators.

Closely related but more complex is the sometimes questionable practice of multiple authors on papers in professional journals. In many fields, especially in the natural sciences, this is a common practice. It is not unusual in some areas for research papers to have as many as four or five or even more authors. Properly conceived, this is entirely legitimate, for joint authorship under these circumstances acknowledges the actual collaboration of several scholars in a particular research project. When all are involved in some substantial way, this practice raises no ethical problems at all.

It is not unknown, however, to see publications in which names have been added even though insubstantial or even no contributions have been made by these ostensible co-authors. Sometimes, the motivation for this practice appears relatively benign. For example, names sometimes are appended as a result of a well-intentioned desire to further a colleague's career. Other times, authors are added in the hope that the name of a widely known and respected academic figure will facilitate publication in a favored journal. In this case, all parties stand to gain, for even the faculty luminary can add yet another research publication to an already impressive record of scholarly productivity.

In this realm, however, not all motivations are well intentioned. Sometimes names appear as joint authors as a result of overt or subtle threats by more powerful members of the academic establishment. Some senior professors in charge of laboratories or research enterprises insist, sometimes to the point of intimidation, that all publications emanating from their operations bear their names - regardless of whether they had any serious input into the specific article or report submitted for publication. This is especially dangerous, and especially pernicious, in the present precarious academic job market. Those whose instincts lead them to resist this form of unethical pressure can easily find themselves out of work and even informally barred from other projects within the senior professor's sphere of influence. In a case reported to me recently, a full professor at UCLA serving as the principal investigator on a grant-funded development project informed the project director that he wanted his name (as co-author) on everything she wrote pertaining to the project. In fact, his involvement in the project had been nominal. When asked to contribute to the actual writing of project-related reports, the full professor declined. When the project director categorically refused his request, he threatened to have her fired. When confronted further, he backed down. There is little reason, unfortunately, to believe that this case is a mere aberration.

Another abuse of the multiple authorship system occurs when virtually everyone in a research project or environment is added, regardless of the specific nature or even existence of their involvement. It is not unknown for papers to be submitted for publication bearing as many as ten or fifteen co-authors. There are times, in fact, when some of these persons have no idea whatever that such a paper has even been written. The sole purpose is clearly to curry personal favor and to allow as many academics as possible to pad their publication lists. Once again, however, this is a form of deception that only adds to the lack of moral rigor in contemporary higher education.

Multiple authorship is sufficiently troublesome that it needs to be much more carefully scrutinized than it has been in the past. Far too many instances of this commonplace academic practice are obviously examples of dubious professional conduct. Intellectual work should be judged solely on its merits and only those who make genuinely substantial contributions to a project should be rewarded with credit for publication. Conduct falling short of that standard should be perceived as a major breach of academic ethics, not unlike plagiarism, falsification of data, or any other overt expression of dishonesty or fraud.

The personal conduct of many academics is another area where there are more ethical breaches and abuses than the profession would care to acknowledge. Deeply rooted in the character and personalities of academic men and women, the attitudes described in Chapter 3 give rise to a vast complex of unsavory practices that are endemic in all large university settings. Like physicians, lawyers, and other professionals, professors often promote a pompous and idealized view of their activities. As a result, many academics treat students, non-academic staff, and junior and marginal academic colleagues in a discourteous and patronizing manner.

Indeed, it would be hard to imagine any institution in which such a rigid hierarchy exists. Because so many professors believe that they, unique among human beings, possess superior intellectual attributes, they treat others who work or study in the university as distinctly inferior. I have already described how students are often viewed contemptuously. Regularly, they are brusquely shunted aside and told to take their concerns to teaching assistants and others more in touch with the academic and other problems of undergraduates. When professors do spend time with students, they often imply that this is a rare privilege and that the students ought to be deeply grateful. In fact, this is nonsense; to spend time with one's students is an obligation of one's job as an educator. To create a context in which it appears to be a grudging descent from more elevated activity is educationally disadvantageous and ultimately unprofessional.

Thousands of university students have internalized these values, thus depriving themselves of educational opportunities to which they are fully entitled. Every week I speak to undergraduates who are fearful of speaking to professors, often even about academic matters directly related to their specific courses. Like patients who are afraid to take the "valuable" time of their physicians by asking detailed questions about their medical conditions, these students have been indoctrinated to respect the false distance imposed among professors and their client population. More poignantly, I observe this phenomenon regularly in my own contact with undergraduates in extremely prosaic situations. Scores of times over the years, for example, I have seen students standing in the hall near my office, evidently confused about something. My usual response is to invite them in and ask if I can help. More often than not, I can provide assistance within a few minutes. Interestingly, I almost always receive profuse thanks, well out of proportion to the very modest help I have rendered. What this suggests about students' ordinary encounters in the large, impersonal university is sad indeed.

More deeply, it reflects a pervasive lack of concern for human feelings, a matter that should also be perceived as within the realm of professional ethics and responsibility.

Some of the most blatantly unethical conduct of academic life occurs in the relationships of professors with non-academic staff, especially with the clerical workers who comprise a large percentage of university employees. Particularly in recent years, I have had substantial opportunity to talk extensively with secretaries, administrative assistants, counselors, and others in non-faculty categories. These conversations have been both profoundly instructive and profoundly dismaying.

An incredible atmosphere of alienation pervades most university settings, a direct consequence of the ways in which so-called "support" personnel are treated by members of the academic staff. I have written in Chapter 3 of the cult of the Ph.D. One tragic byproduct of this attitude is that clerical and similar employees are often viewed as inferior in intelligence and thus defective as human beings. In many academic settings, there are powerful informal rules against fraternizing with support personnel. Consistent breaches of this convention can label a faculty member as odd or even untrustworthy and can have subtly negative implications for advancement up the academic ladder.

Probably the most troublesome feature of faculty-staff relationships can be seen in the way in which work is delegated. It is no exaggeration to note that many secretaries are treated as little more than extensions of office furniture. In my experience, this is a ubiquitous and well justified complaint that is worsened because so many professors have no genuine idea of what they are really doing. I have observed professors as they approach a secretary, drop a pile of work on her desk, and walk away without even a word of conversation. In addition, far too many professors are demanding to the point of cruelty. I have seen faculty members literally scream at clerical workers if they find a few typographical errors or if a deadline (often an unreasonable deadline) has not been met.

Unfortunately, there is more to this disgraceful pattern of human interaction. Many professors view non-academic employees as veritable servants whose role is to cater to their every need, whether serious or trivial. A common practice is to instruct clerical workers to perform even the most mundane administrative acts such as filling out a book order list or

123

putting a library book on reserve or even placing telephone calls. The point, of course, is that many professors perceive such tasks as beneath their dignity, and they make that abundantly clear as they delegate the particular task. More insidious still is when purely personal affairs are handed cavalierly to clerical employees. Far too many academics believe that as professors, they have every right to expect that secretaries should make their dinner reservations, change their children's dental appointments, or arrange to have their tires rotated. Accompanying all of this is the constant reminder, expressed both verbally and non-verbally, that those at the lower end of the hierarchy must be eternally cognizant of their status.

All of these indignities have been experienced by clerical workers throughout the country and throughout the world. Universities again are identical in one respect to most other organizations and institutions. The sad reality is that a pattern of immorality - more modest and tactful language would be inappropriate - exists virtually everywhere. This unsavory human conduct invariably causes immense problems of morale. In university settings this has a dampening effect on all academic functions, especially educational. Often, for example, frustrated clerical personnel in turn treat students inappropriately, thus reinforcing heirarchial values that are inimical to educational cooperation.

Strikingly similar attitudes and actions are present in the relationships between established professors and the marginal faculty members on whom much of a university's instructional load actually falls. During the past decade, when the academic job market has fallen to a catastrophic state, thousands of itinerant instructors, many of whom are recently-graduated Ph.D.'s (and many of whom are women), have been hired to teach introductory courses in hundreds of universities. Desperate for work and inexpensively employed, they are easy targets for exploitation. Denied many employment benefits and the possibility for promotion, the best that they can hope for is a few years of academic employment and a letter or two of good recommendations, before they move on to a similar situation in another institution - if they are lucky. Even more than teaching assistants or untenured junior faculty, they are as vulnerable to degrading and unprofessional treatment as any group of workers in the United States.

This situation is nothing less than scandalous today. I have spoken at great length to many of these academic migrants and I have closely observed the ways they are treated by "regular" faculty members in the modern university. In some basic respects, they are treated little differently from clerical employees. Above all, they are constantly reminded of their own marginality and of their inflexible status as second-class academic citizens. Such reminders are rarely overt. Rather, they are expressed in those powerful forms of non-verbal communication that extract a psychic toll far more painful than more open forms of hostility or contempt.

Specific examples abound in modern universities. Generally these temporary faculty members are relegated to outlying offices, frequently having to share such quarters with several other persons in the same precarious postion. Sometimes the academic department neglects to provide mailboxes for them in the main office. Typically, they are not listed in official university publications as members of the faculty. They rarely receive internal department and institutional memoranda, are scarcely ever consulted on matters of policy, and are generally not invited to faculty meetings and similar official gatherings.

Treatment on more personal levels is often equally disgraceful. In the past few years, I have seen this phenomenon intimately at UCLA. On that campus is a special writing program employing over thirty men and women as faculty members whose mission is to train undergraduates to communicate more effectively in writing. Most of these faculty are young, most have doctoral degrees, and most are very good at what they do. Several, in fact, are quite exceptional and are, I believe, the intellectual superiors of many professors holding tenured positions at UCLA. All members of the writing program's faculty are classified as "Visiting Lecturers" and are limited to a maximum number of years of faculty service in that category. Tenure is thus unavailable regardless of their accomplishments. These young instructors are classically marginal, relegated to inferior status within the academic hierarchy.

In extensive personal conversations, I have heard their complaints regularly. A recurring theme is that they are simply ignored by the regular tenure-track faculty. When they are invited to parties at all, they are forced to converse with each other, for many regular professors are either uncomfortable in their presence or feel that conversation with such marginal academics is unworthy of their more elevated claims to professional respectability. Similarly, in departmental offices and in the corridors of academic buildings, senior professors pass them by, with little or no regard even for the canons of common courtesy. With equal regularity, they are mistaken for teaching assistants rather than as professionals performing high level, sophisticated academic functions. This callously mistaken assumption in turn encourages regular faculty members to view them with the same smugness that characterizes their social intercourse with all inferior categories of academic personnel.

This situation is hardly confined to the Los Angeles campus of the University of California. Throughout the nation there are thousands of other migrant academic workers who are subtly denied recognition of their own identities as teachers and scholars. Despite the official rhetoric among the academic establishment that this is deplorable and unacceptable, there is little evidence to conclude that such concern transcends the verbal level. My own speculation is that emotionally, this situation in fact is very gratifying to far too many senior professors. Given their powerful insecurities and their overwhelming need to express their own supposed intellectual superiority, the existence of this academic underclass provides them with further ammunition for their delusionary concerns. This too must be perceived in ethical terms; the way that people in power deal with people of lesser rank and status is a matter of profound moral significance. Once more, conduct falling short of reasonableness is unprofessional and should not be tolerated in academic life.

Further examination suggests that even more unethical practices emerge from time to time in American universities. Professors are not immune, for example, from traditional attitudes of racial and sexual prejudice. On one level, of course, university faculty members are far more liberal on such issues than the majority of the population in the United States. Many university professors have been active in civil rights struggles. Many have been equally active in campus efforts to make educational opportunities more available to racial and ethnic minority groups that have historically been excluded from the benefits of higher education. The admirable efforts of some, however, are far from universal. There is still substantial resistance in prestigious universities to affirmative action for students, staff, and faculty. Too many professors continue to treat minority group members patronizingly and paternalisticly. And occasionally in the private conversations among academics, overt expressions of racist ideas emerge. Although racism is not the primary problem in modern university life, conversations with black and Latino students, staff, and faculty reveal that there is a long distance to go before democratic ideals are consistent with daily academic realities.

The problem of sexism in contemporary higher education is somewhat more complex. Historically, universities have been bastions of male domination. Although significant changes have occurred in recent years, attitudes that are so deeply ingrained do not dissipate easily. It is sadly apparent that women students, employees, and even academic colleagues are frequently maligned and mistreated by weak, resentful male faculty members and administrators. Thousands of male professors assume, whether consciously or not, that women have little place in the tough, masculine world of the intellect. As a direct result of such irrational and unprofessional attitudes, women are compelled to carry additional burdens in their own academic lives.

Typically, sexist attitudes and actions are more subtle than overt. As in so many other features of university life, they are communicated non-verbally, for more blatant manifestations would be considered unseemly in the final decades of the twentieth century. A major example can be seen in the reactions of many male professors to women's studies courses and programs and to feminist scholarship. Whether they are prepared to admit it or not, the attitude is often that such enterprises are ultimately less than serious, a transient fashion that deflects attention from "real" academic business. Intellectual efforts along feminist lines tend to be subtly devalued in the councils of academic power. Women scholars working in this developing tradition often find their opportunities and prospects for promotion diminished. When their publications are negatively reviewed, the formal terminology employed is likely the verbal shorthand for the more primal tendencies of patriarchal domination.

More than most other professionals, academics create a clubby atmosphere that pervades the daily operations of the institution. Especially in the most prestigious research universities, an "old boy" spirit exerts a powerful influence on the major decision-making processes. Like blacks and Latinos, women fit uneasily into a scheme whose historical roots are so deep and whose emotional sources are so poorly understood by the participants themselves. The tangible effects are obvious. Women employees dominate the clerical workforce, and they are regarded as the equivalents of traditional housewives and nurses. At the faculty level, women are highly concentrated at the lower end of the academic ladder and in the ranks of irregular and marginal academic workers. Universities have in general responded grudgingly and sluggishly to affirmative action demands. Women are strikingly underrepresented in many academic fields and in many university departments, notwithstanding that they comprise the majority of graduate students in some of these areas. When pressed for explanations, male professors usually complain about the lack of qualified female scholars and the need to preserve "standards" and maintain "excellence." Again, however, such expressions are often code words that conceal a powerful inability and unwillingness to live in a world of authentic sexual equality.

More ominous are the periodic episodes of sexual misconduct that occur on university campuses in America. The women's movement has finally been successful in bringing the problem of sexual harassment to public attention. For too many years, this degrading and immoral phenomenon was ignored and denied, in schools, universities, factories, offices, and elsewhere. In the late 1970's, however, a proliferation of articles and books on this topic made it clear that a large percentage of women have been subjected to the emotionally disruptive and coercive sexual advances of males holding positions of superior power in organizational settings.

This literature was instrumental in proving that academic life was no exception to a widespread pattern of unprofessional conduct. Women students and employees, however, have been painfully aware that they are subject to a vast complex of reprisals (or, more insidiously, to the threat of reprisals) if they resist the sexual demands of male administrators, supervisors, professors, and teaching assistants. It is important to understand this in human rather than abstract or statistical terms. Since I began teaching in 1967, I have spoken to a large number of sexual harassment victims, mostly upper-division and graduate level students. Conservatively, I have heard fifty or sixty personal accounts of some of the most grotesque and disgusting conduct that can exist in an academic institution. I should add that I have utterly no reason to doubt the authenticity of these accounts. In most of my conversations with these victims of sexual harassment, a high level of emotional anxiety and tension has been obvious, an inevitable result of the monstrous conduct to which they have been subjected.

The experiences of these women have run the gamut of sexual improprieties. Frequently, they have been the recipients of verbal sexual suggestions or solicitations from male instructional personnel. Equally often, they have had to deal with overt sexual leering, accompanied by lewd jokes revealing deeply held sexist biases and attitudes. Several students have reported that they have been fondled, rubbed, pinched, and kissed unexpectedly. Most perniciously, many have been promised high grades or favorable references in exchange for carnal favors, with the clearest implication that refusal would result in mediocre grades, inferior recommendations, or termination of employment.

Two comparatively recent examples brought to my attention provide a concrete sense of the ugly realities of sexual harassment. In the first case, an upper-level history student with strong accomplishments in that field was invited to do an independent research project for academic credit with a prominent professor. Flattered at this recognition of her intellectual abilities, she embarked upon her work with enthusiasm. Throughout the academic term, she received positive feedback from the professor, which served to fortify her own self-confidence. In due course, she was invited to have coffee with the professor, ostensibly to discuss her academic project. When they met, she was surprised to hear him discuss his personal problems. He told her that he was dissatisfied with his marriage and that he was desperately lonely. He mentioned his feeling of emotional and sexual attractiveness for the student and suggested that they spend time together. Shocked, horrified, and tremendously upset, she terminated the meeting and shortly withdrew from the research project. The next time she saw the professor, he crossed the street in order to avoid eye contact.

In the second case, an undergraduate female student had been involved in a national organization for honors students. Having been elected to the governing board of the association, she worked closely with other students and faculty members from throughout the country. Among other things, this entailed travel to various board meetings and to regional and national gatherings of the organization. At one of the latter conferences, she worked with a distinguished male professor on a series of association policy changes that both thought would be advantageous. One evening, the professor telephoned her at her room in the hotel in which the conference was held. He asked to see her, ostensibly to discuss various organizational matters. Shortly after his arrival in her room, he began to fondle her and express his desire for a sexual liaison. Like the student in the first case, she was horrified and distraught. She too broke off contact with the professor after this immoral encounter.

The educational implications of such unprofessional actions are no less awesome and horrendous than the emotional consequences to the victims. Faculty members who deal with students on the basis of personal sexual indulgence make a mockery of the university ideals of merit and intellectual standards. Male professors who debase these legitimate ideals typically enjoy an enormous power advantage over their female victims. They determine the academic rewards and sanctions and they have the power to influence future careers through recommendations and personal contacts.

This must be understood, furthermore, in an historical and social context in which women have received minimal encouragement or support for pursuing intellectual goals. Sexual harassment almost inevitably has a profoundly negative effect upon a woman's confidence. Every victim to whom I have spoken has wondered whether her academic success was authentic or whether she was rewarded simply because of her physical attributes. In many cases, their commitment to continue their scholarly efforts has come under severe strain. The educational results of this form of academic immorality are thus nothing short of brutal.

It is time for disconcerting candor on this score. Such things do exist, and they are not as rare as professors and university administrators would like the public to believe. Each year scandals are cleverly or clumsily concealed by department chairmen and other officials. But no cover-up can negate the patent immorality of exchanging academic rewards for sexual surrenders or of treating human beings as casual sexual objects. The perpetrators of such conduct have no more right to continue as academics than the Watergate criminals had to continue in the practice of law.

The past decade has also seen an increased public concern with the business and consulting activities of increasing numbers of university professors. Recent dramatic examples of faculty members, especially in bio-technology fields, transforming their research discoveries into multi-million dollar business enterprises have made many people wonder about conflicts of interest. This problem has also evoked serious concern at the highest levels of university administration. University presidents from Harvard, the University of California, the Massachusetts Institute of Technology and comparable institutions have met in order to determine how to handle the problem of commercially profitable research results and products conducted in university facilities on university time.

Conflict of interest is indeed an issue of deep ethical concern in the modern university. There are professors whose activities as university employees (for which they are fully and often handsomely paid) are thoroughly subordinate to their external business interests. For these persons, university affiliation is an advantageous mechanism for the pursuit of private pecuniary concerns. Most faculty members involved in this conduct are actually small businesspersons operating modest enterprises out of their faculty offices or laboratories. Typically, they run computer software companies, arrange real estate transactions, perform lab tests for individuals and small firms, organize modest publishing enterprises, and engage in a variety of similar commercial activities. With the rarest exceptions, they are far removed from the realm of high finance and multi-national corporate operations.

The scope and scale of these university-based and assisted profit-making activities have little to do, however, with their moral status. Professors involved in these enterprises are exploiting their privileged professional positions. The fruits of their labors bring no benefits or advantages to the university, but only augment personal income. These businesses detract from all aspects of university responsibilities because they demand time and emotional energy that could be directed towards proper professional obligations. The specifically educational consequences are self-evident. A faculty member pursuing a personal business deal on university time is less likely to spend extra time with undergraduate students. Neither is he or she likely to resist the temptation to cut corners in order to save time in course preparation, evaluation of student work, or other functions demanded of instructional personnel.

It is important to recognize that this particular form of ethically dubious conduct is a natural by-product of the values of the modern multiversity. The entrepreneurial ambiance in this institution is so pervasive that it colors virtually all operations and functions. In due course it also conditions personal attitudes. It encourages *per se* the value of individual initiative in securing financial advantage, to the point where it is almost incidental whether such monetary advancement emerges from successful grant proposals or university subsidized private businesses. With his familiar blend of impressive insightfulness and extreme tolerance, Clark Kerr noted the existence of the professor-entrepreneur over twenty years ago:

> He [the professor] may even become, as some have, essentially a professional man with his home office and basic retainer on the campus of the multiversity but with his clients scattered from coast to coast.[4]

A significant but morally ambiguous feature of this general phenomenon is the wide range of consulting activities performed by university professors. This is extremely commonplace today, especially in the nation's most distinguished research institutions. Faculty members in all fields, save perhaps a few humanities disciplines, have the opportunity to provide personal services for the government, for foundations, for private corporations and businesses, for school districts, for professional groups and associations, for other institutions of higher education, or for anyone else seeking short-term advice from suitable academic experts. For many academics, particularly in such fields as management, law, medicine, engineering, education, psychology, and other natural and social sciences, consulting fees add considerably to their yearly incomes.

Properly limited, there is nothing wrong or unprofessional about this enterprise. Consulting, in fact, can help keep professors professionally alive and engaged at high levels of accomplishment. It can enable professors to connect their research findings and intellectual theories to concrete human problems. A valuable result of this connection, of course, can be improved classroom instruction. Finally, there are valuable public service implications arising out of some consulting activities. The university has important obligations to the rest of society, and the deployment of its faculty personnel in addressing and solving major social and technological problems is ordinarily mutually beneficial.

The ethical problems in this area emerge when faculty consulting obligations begin to overpower the regular professional commitments required by university employment. Regrettably, this is not uncommon. For some faculty members, consulting practices have become so lucrative that more of their annual incomes derive from this source than from their university salaries. Under these circumstances, they are inclined to slight their regular duties in favor of more profitable external activity. Faculty members holding tenured positions are in an excellent position to abuse their trust in this fashion. By teaching the same courses again and again and by avoiding the ordinary committee and similar obligations of faculty life, they can reduce their university work to a few hours a week. Since their university employment is secure, they can feel perfectly safe even if they produce minimal research.

The educational consequences are both familiar and deplorable. An excessive devotion to private consulting not only encourages stale and repetitive courses and instruction, but more subtly diminishes the value and priority of the entire range of educational activities. Classes and office hours, for example, are frequently cancelled because they conflict with a consulting contract. Routine obligations become easy targets for neglect, and consulting requirements are slowly transformed from adjunct professional activity to matters of primary personal significance. This too occurs far more frequently than university authorities would be comfortable in acknowledging.[5]

All of the preceding do not exhaust the range of professional misconduct in contemporary university affairs. It points, however, to a need to create mechanisms to reduce and prevent these ethical misdeeds. There is no easy path, of course, to accomplish this objective. Above all, there needs to be a profound change in attitude and consciousness throughout the institutions of higher learning in America. The topics of faculty ethics and professional responsibility need to become matters of the highest priority. The daily routines and conduct of professors need to be scrutinized as much for their ethical character as for their intellectual excellence. Without such a change in institutional consciousness, education will continue to be a cruel hoax, an effort considerably inferior in importance to those activities that give rise to enormous professional misconduct.

One potentially valuable first step in addressing the ethical problems of academic life would be the creation of a carefully constructed code of ethics for academic personnel. Such a code is no panacea, for as the lawyers have shown, formal rules and principles hardly guarantee ethical conduct. Valuable benefits, however, could conceivably ensue. The primary advantage of a detailed formal ethical code is that it would encourage academics to treat the entire issue of professional responsibility more seriously than they have in the past. A clear statement of what is expected of a professor, moreover, would make it easier to take effective action when abuses occur. At present, there is considerable reluctance to proceed against offending faculty members because guidelines are vague or even non-existent. A code of academic conduct, clearly drawn and contractually binding, might reduce this reluctance. The beneficiaries would be the entire academic community.

An institutionalized commitment to professional responsibility would have even broader educational and social consequences. A university where faculty members take special care to act properly at every level of their professional lives will be far more conducive to education and the advancement of knowledge. Furthermore, an academic profession that provides ethical as well as intellectual leadership can properly exert an influence throughout society as a whole.

No code of conduct is valuable without adequate enforcement procedures. Morally uplifting rhetoric is no substitute for firm action, and suitable sanctions are clearly necessary for violations of professional ethics. At present, there are virtually no effective penalties for professors discovered in breach of their ethical obligations. Disciplinary proceedings are so rare as to be laughable. I know of only a handful of cases in more than nineteen years of university teaching. Appropriate mechanisms, consistent with applicable standards of due process, can legitimize such consequences as reprovals, fines, suspensions, and even dismissals. Unpleasant as this may be, it is sometimes necessary, for academics are similar to other human beings. When their offending colleagues are punished for their indiscretions, a powerful deterrent effect is likely to be created.

Professors have, as I suggested earlier in this chapter, a remarkable ability to apply their intellectual acuity in every conceivable direction in the natural and social worlds. The time has come for a modest redirection of this capacity toward the internal dynamics of the university itself. A continuation of this dangerous dualism, where only the affairs of others are fit subjects for critical inquiry, is both foolish and shortsighted. Even more basically, it is a negation of the very intellectual values that are supposed to comprise the soul of the academic enterprise.

NOTES

1. George Howe Colt, "Too Good to be True," Harvard Magazine, July-August, 1983, pp.22-23.

2. Ibid., p.23.

3. Ibid., p.24.

4. Clark Kerr, *The Uses of the University* (Cambridge, Massachusetts: Harvard University Press, 1963), p.44.

5. There is another dimension to the problem of the consulting practices of university faculty members. For many professionals, including academics, knowledge and expertise are considered neutral and value-free. The ends to which such knowledge is directed may be good or bad, but the expertise itself carries no such connotation. This view, of course, is extremely convenient, for it allows experts to avoid confronting the social and political implications of their work and discoveries. It is reasonable, however, to inquire into the ethics of a psychologist who advises an advertising company on how to manipulate people to buy cigarettes or an economist who counsels a corporation to pay damage claims for personal injuries instead of retooling in order to prevent accidents in the first place. This is a complex issue that goes far beyond the scope of the present book.

CHAPTER 6

Student Complicity in Educational Mediocrity

For the reasons elaborated in the previous five chapters, I have concluded that mediocrity dominates the educational affairs of America's prestigious research universities. A misplaced scheme of values and priorities has been rigidly established, making the modern university as resistant to change as any comparable institution. With the rarest exceptions, professors are rewarded for their published research along conventional lines and penalized for a serious dedication to undergraduate education. This is a reality that professors and administrators will acknowledge in private, although they are understandably reluctant to be as candid for public attribution.

This arrangement, as I have argued throughout this book, encourages intellectual narrowness and discourages effective teaching, a result that reinforces the emotional predilictions of the large majority of university faculty members. The ultimate losers are the undergraduate students, whose baccalaureate degrees conceal the fact that they are marginally educated and programmed to become passive and uncritical members of society. The social, political, and cultural implications of this result are nothing less than horrifying. No society is well served by a citizenry oriented to adaptation and ill equipped to offer intelligent and creative solutions to the vast social and economic problems of modern life.

It is fruitless to isolate any one segment of the university community for blame in this disconcerting state of affairs. The reasons are enormously complex, and each element plays a role that reinforces the whole. As I have shown, it would be foolish to ignore the fundamental responsibility of the faculty. Professors have been instrumental in creating the institutional setting that is so congenial to their inclinations, despite their habitual whining about present academic difficulties. The blunt fact is that the large majority of faculty men and women are prepared to tolerate educational mediocrity as long as scholarly reputations and careerist rewards are available without serious instructional commitment.

Administrative authorities abet this problem by formalizing and legitimizing these faculty priorities. University bureaucrats contribute to the low status of education by their empire-building propensities and by their own career agendas that scarcely depend on any genuine commitment to instructional change and improvement. Both groups, professors and administrators, reinforce this structure of values and practices by their awesome success in hiring, retaining, and promoting those who, in perfect justice, can be considered clones of themselves.

There is, unfortunately, another major element that must be considered in any overall understanding of the educational failures of the modern university. With sadness, I have concluded that undergraduate students themselves are a significant factor in the inadequate nature of higher education today. Notwithstanding that they are the primary victims of dominant institutional values and policies, their passivity and indifference only exacerbate the sources of their own oppression. It is time to recognize candidly that student attitudes and actions are far from perfect. In fact, an insidious combination of apathy, ignorance, and selfishness on the part of thousands of students supports the pervasive pattern of educational mediocrity. In order to truly understand what is wrong with American universities, these disturbing realities must be explored in depth.

At the outset of such an analysis, it must be reiterated that students are hardly the major cause of defective undergraduate education. Failure to realize that could lead, all too easily, to the dangerous phenomenon of blaming the victim, an analytic mode in American life (and sometimes in American scholarship) that has too often polluted both the intellectual and political atmospheres in this country. The point, however, is that student values contribute to a vicious circle that diminishes the prospects for effective undergraduate education and reduces the possibilities for serious reform. This phenomenon is complicity in the classic sense of that term. It is a complicity in educational mediocrity that is rarely understood and easily ignored, by students no less than anyone else. It is vital to examine this reality as concretely as possible.

Before detailing some of the specific manifestations, I want to indicate why I find student complicity in educational mediocrity so disturbing. In my own career, I have come to have enormous affection for most of the students I have served at the University of California and elsewhere. Because close student contact is a source of personal and professional satisfaction to me, I have had thousands of extended conversations with undergraduates over the years. My view that they are fundamentally neglected and bureaucratically abused has led me frequently to intervene on their behalf. Regularly, I have urged students to respond assertively to an academic system that marks them as largely incidental to its operations. When instead I see a resigned acceptance of these realities and attitudes that only make them even more entrenched, I feel a genuine sense of despair. Nevertheless, it is important to be as critical about the student population as anything else in academic institutions.

At the risk of overgeneralization, I perceive the present generation of university students as far from impressive. I make this judgment, obviously, on the basis of my own extensive experiences as a front-line teacher and on what I believe to be reliable reports from academic colleagues throughout the country. My impression is that a disturbingly large percentage of contemporary university undergraduates lack intellectual curiosity, broad vision, and moral sensitivity. Although I have had the personal pleasure of having an extremely high percentage of students of immense intelligence and integrity, it is obvious that these young men and women are exceptional and generally unrepresentative of the vast majority of their contemporaries.

It has been widely reported, of course, that today's university students are extremely different from their counterparts of the activist 1960's. Anyone with university experience spanning this entire time would be constrained to agree, at least at a broad and general level. My students in the late 1960's were usually better prepared and more amenable to educational risk and experimentation than my students in the 1980's. Moreover, they were far more receptive to a critical view of social and political life and displayed a far greater commitment to social and ethical concerns transcending the pleasures and demands of private life. And while they were hardly indifferent to their future career and employment plans, they were not obsessed with these realities in contrast to hundreds of thousands of university students in 1986.

Political and economic conditions have changed drastically. The war in Viet Nam is over, eliminating the major source of student moral outrage and political involvement. The economic uncertainties of the late 1970's and early 1980's have made it inevitable that contemporary students would be nervous and insecure about their employment prospects and futures. It is necessary too to avoid a deceptively romantic view of the students of the 1960's. They were also far from perfect. For all too many, their social idealism was as fashionable as the present infatuation with designer clothing. Regrettably, much of the objection to the war involved a sense that it could be dangerous to personal safety or inconvenient to future plans. Educationally, the widespread demand that university courses be made immediately "relevant" to social concerns and personal feelings was often shortsighted and disastrous. Still, it was a more exciting era that at least raised the promise that university life could be reformed along humane and progressive lines.

My observations today convince me that student attitudes both reflect and fortify dominant institutional realities. In the face of indifferent and uninspiring teaching and a marginal university commitment to undergraduate education generally, many students respond by encouraging an even further erosion of academic rigor and intellectual breadth. In order to pursue studies that are comfortable and undemanding, large numbers of students opt for the safety and security of narrow specialization. They eagerly absorb the values of specific academic disciplines and erect psychological barriers against the instrusions of other approaches and interdisciplinary syntheses. Students in the humanities and social sciences typically complain mightily about having to do modest coursework in mathematics and the natural sciences. With equal ignorance, natural science students whine about wasting time in such "useless" enterprises as philosophy, English literature, ancient history, and foreign language classes. They seek an education compatible with their immediate and narrow inclinations, worrying far more about grades than about the actual content and analytic training to be derived from enrollment in university programs.

The implications are both obvious and dangerous. Non-science students who expect to meet the responsibilities of life in the twenty first century need to know something about science and technology. To avoid these subjects because they are hard, unpleasant, or more frequently, dangerous to the maintenance of a high grade-point average is a classic example of immaturity and false economy. Engineering and science students who avoid the humanities for similar reasons increase the likelihood that they will emerge as what Ortega y Gasset called technically competent "barbarians."[1] In neither case are the students well served. More importantly, society is particularly ill served by a student population that cannot be considered truly educated in any meaningful sense of that term. What is especially tragic about all this shortsightedness is that it is little different from the attitudes of professors who immerse themselves in scholarly esoterica at the expense of a broader vision. Narrowness begets narrowness, and the misplaced values of the university faculty pass with ease to much of the student body. That both groups suffer from severe intellectual tunnel vision is hardly accidental. It is, on the contrary, an inevitable consequence of the modern multiversity and its organization, values, and selection of its primary personnel.

Every week I see the clearest examples of this powerful unwillingness to take intellectual risks by exploring areas of human knowledge beyond one's personal abilities and inclinations. Instead of seeing new fields as exciting challenges, they are viewed as impediments to personal advancement. With unnerving regularity, I observe students opting for enrollment in courses with mechanistic memorization obligations instead of demands for serious and synthetic thought. Often, students will select courses with multiple choice examinations instead of research or argumentative written requirements. Most commonly, they seek classes known to be amenable to minimal effort in pursuit of high grades guaranteeing ultimate admission to law, medical, and management schools and the like. Some of these attitudes, unfortunately, can be traced to the excess of the

1960's, when many universities surrendered to student demands to eliminate virtually all academic requirements.

In fairness, I should note that some university faculty members and administrators have been disturbed by excessive student laziness and intellectual myopia. Ever since Harvard reinstituted distribution and general education requirements a few years ago, many institutions have followed suit. Increasingly today, students are required to enroll in courses beyond their own areas in order to achieve at least some minimal intellectual breadth during their undergraduate years. While these recent changes should be generally applauded, they will remain intrinsically superficial and limited as long as they are not accompanied by major changes in institutional priorities. An educational policy that consists of little more than imposing requirements on undergraduates means very little without a broader university commitment to exploring and communicating the relationships between various fields of knowledge and various modes of intellectual inquiry.

There are several other features of student attitudes and values that contribute to a mediocre university environment. For example, there is an amazing ignorance among undergraduates today, including among those who have done spectacularly well in high school and who are enrolled in prestigious universities. Virtually any classroom teacher can note that many students know very little about the things that most educated people take for granted. In my own classes, for example, it is no longer possible to make historical allusions that go back more than a decade or so. In upper level courses at UCLA, I have regularly discovered students who have never heard of Dwight Eisenhower or the Cuban Missile Crisis. The mention of such literary figures as Franz Kafka or even Leo Tolstoy frequently evokes blank stares. I know that I am no exception in these discoveries.

The absence of factual information is no educational catastrophe. Facts can be learned and in any case they are only a small part of a serious educational operation. What is troubling is that such ignorance is too often joined by a powerful indifference. I have talked regularly to students who acknowledge their ignorance at the same time that they express no concern or dismay at this state of affairs. On the contrary, I have heard students say that they have no motivation to learn

142

things they believe have little relevance to their daily lives. Too many are deeply apathetic and complacent about their own lack of knowledge. An inadequate commitment to education in American universities probably makes this inevitable. Unfortunately, this widespread fusion of ignorance and apathy has insidious consequences, not the least of which is that it discourages faculty members and administrators from embarking on systematic efforts at educational change and improvement.

Closely related is a pervasive selfishness that seems to dominate the consciousness of most contemporary undergraduates. This is a reflection of a more national mood of narcissism that several prominent commentators such as Christopher Lasch and Richard Sennett have noted during the past decade. Its most obvious manifestation among students is an indifference toward public obligations and an elevation of interest in personal advancement and private life. At UCLA, for example, a speech by Ralph Nader might draw a few score socially conscious students. An appearance by Joan Rivers or Cher, on the other hand, usually draws an overflow crowd of thousands. A forum on American involvement in Central America will evoke the interest of fewer than fifty students. A seminar on dressing for success, however, will itself be a smashing success.

The educational manifestations are more subtle. Courses are selected on the basis of personal expediency as much as intellectual interest. Beyond the choice of classes that are easily graded and cognitively undemanding, a major criterion is whether the instructor will be a good reference source for professional school or prospective employers. Furthermore, students increasingly select courses that they believe will be practical in their quest for success in business and the professions. Western civilization and advanced French literature thus give way to courses in accounting and computer science. While I will show later why this is a bogus and deluded view of practicality, the point here is that the motivation is selfishly based. The existence of these values only contributes to an undistinguished educational environment in even the top universities in the United States today.

An equally troubling characteristic of contemporary student attitudes is a strong and sometimes mechanistic conservatism.

143

By this, I do not mean a thoughtful adherence to the conservative tradition in politics and philosophy. Rather, I have observed an emotional commitment to the status quo, whatever it happens to be at any moment. It appears as an ingrained fearfulness about change, a manifestation, I believe, of an unhealthy and uncharacteristic concern with security among young adults. Often enough, my students will concur with the view that all is not perfect in the world of society and politics. They are astute enough to understand that injustice abounds and that millions of people are victimized by oppressive institutional forces. At the same time, however, they often express the concern that any attempted changes would only make things worse and, more revealingly, disruptive and uncomfortable. This powerful psychic commitment to stability as an end in itself prevents students from fully understanding how the university serves them poorly and how they themselves reinforce this pattern of educational mediocrity.

It is difficult to totally understand the sources of this prediliction toward extreme caution. In part, it appears to be a response to the deep uncertainties of the times. In part, it may also be a reaction to the turmoil of the 1960's and early 1970's. From my extensive conversations with students in recent years, it appears as well to be an uncritical reflection of parental attitudes and fears. In any case, however, it is a frightening phenomenon whose implications go far beyond the failures of higher education. If indeed an entire generation of young people is so fearful of change and instability, the nation more generally will pay a high price far into the future.

Another major reality of modern student life has been widely reported in the mass media during the 1970's and early 1980's. It is no secret that millions of American university students are concerned almost exclusively with their future employment prospects. It is understandable that the current economic uncertainty should generate a massive concern with the relationships of undergraduate education to the job market. The problem is that this has become obsessive. For many students, this is an almost exclusive topic of conversation. In many instances, there are strong undertones of desperation. In hundreds of conversations with students, I have the impression that they feel that they are candidates for a lifetime of economic insecurity.

This preoccupation is basically absurd. The large majority of my students at Berkeley and UCLA have been relatively intelligent white, upper middle class citizens. They will doubtless experience some difficulties in achieving their professional and economic objectives. Jobs are hardly plentiful today and entry into such professions as law and medicine is no longer a guarantee of immense personal affluence. Many will find, especially in the years following their graduations, that their employment prospects are shaky and that they will have to be geographically flexible.

What they fail to realize, however, is that upper middle class graduates of prestigious universities fare much better than less fortunate citizens. The people in the most precarious position are working class men and women and members of traditionally oppressed minority groups. For all its severity, the current economic crisis has a far more modest impact on university students and graduates than on others in America. The current obsession among students about employment is therefore intellectually dubious and morally insensitive.

This excessive concern with jobs, however, generates a variety of unfortunate results in academic settings. There has been a large increase in savage competition, a major reduction in human compassion, and a widespread disregard for the potential and value of a serious general education. These consequences reveal a dramatic manifestation of student complicity in educational mediocrity.

This narrow employment focus among university students is yet another counterpart to dominant institutional values. Thousands of professors, of course, view their own careers as the sole focus of the academic enterprise. They too are keenly aware of the tight academic job market. Faculty selfishness virtually guarantees that a broader and more beneficial undergraduate program will fail to emerge. The same pattern is repeated: selfishness begets more selfishness, and education suffers monumentally. The inadequacies of one constituent element of the university are thus reinforced by the inadequacies of another. Students, who rarely perceive how intimately this process can affect them, probably suffer the most serious consequences of all.

As noted earlier, the student preoccupation with future employment has led to an intense desire to replace the liberal arts curriculum with courses and programs of more "practical" value. While I have argued that the present curriculum is profoundly defective, the substitution of supposedly practical, vocationally oriented courses would be, I believe, catastrophic. Today's students, however, seem intent upon enrolling in business administration, engineering, computer science, and similar courses that they believe will be advantageous to their future careers. Many, in fact, would dispense with the entire liberal arts tradition if they could learn the secrets of marketing recreational vehicles or the ways to succeed in the fashion industry.

This ignorant and at times contemptuous attitude towards liberal learning is deeply disturbing. There is profound value in the liberal arts tradition. To understand the past and to come to grips with the great ideas and discoveries in the major fields of human endeavor is not only exciting in itself, but it can enrich life in every respect. It can promote a lifelong intellectual curiosity that can be both useful and gratifying. It can foster better judgment and increase cultural and aesthetic sensitivity. The logical, analytic, and communication skills, furthermore, that emerge from the liberal arts tradition are remarkably valuable in human affairs. To eschew these benefits in favor of transitory techniques is a classic example of false economy.

Ironically, these purportedly "practical" alternatives turn out, on closer scrutiny, to be not necessarily very practical at all. In the past several years, I have spoken to enough prospective employers to conclude that they prefer men and women with basic analytic and communication strengths and a broad understanding of the social and natural worlds. Specific job tasks are generally learned on the job anyway, and many employers prefer to assume that responsibility themselves. Furthermore, many of the "practical" skills learned in university classes in 1986 may well be obsolete in 1996. The rapid development of technology in America suggests that it would be wise to remain skeptical about what appears to be practical today. The basic skills fostered by the best traditions of liberal learning enable human beings to remain flexible and adapt to new social and economic conditions. A genuine reformation of undergraduate education along such lines would be the most practical policy of all.

Most professors and university administrators share these sentiments, at least abstractly. Their passive and defeatist attitudes in the face of this vocational and "practical" onslaught is therefore disconcerting. More insidious still is the subtle transformation of liberal arts courses and curricula into vocational preparation enterprises, a process that panders to present attitudes and that further devalues the liberal arts tradition. If the abolition of course requirements and the reduction of intellectual standards were inappropriate responses to the student demands of the 1960's, the present response is at least equally inappropriate. In both cases, educational mediocrity is strengthened at the expense of a more demanding and useful educational vision.

Student competition generated by today's job-oriented undergraduates intensifies the educational problems in contemporary university life. Almost all front-line university teachers are aware of the intense competitive environment among students. This process approaches the level of savagery as students try to outflank each other in order to gain real or imagined advantages. Some will do almost anything to secure an "A," believing that only a near-perfect grade-point average can bring admission to prestigious professional schools and thus "success" in life. I have seen students literally beg for higher grades, imploring me or my colleagues to reconsider a decision to award a less than perfect mark. Without exaggeration, I have heard students cry to the point of hysteria, some having commented that their grade of "B" (on a few occasions even a grade of "A-") is one of the major tragedies of their lives. Sadly, while such cases are unusual, they are only the extreme manifestation of all too common attitudes.

Inevitably, such extreme competitiveness bordering on neurosis has ethical implications. Student cheating has always been a problem in higher education, but it appears to have intensified in recent years. Stories about pre-medical students, for example, are legion. Allegedly, it has become commonplace for pre-meds to alter or destroy the lab results of fellow students in key biology and chemistry classes, thus elevating their own position on the grading curve. Enough of my own pre-medical students have assured me that this is true that I have no reason to disbelieve it. Similar stories about other forms of student misconduct also abound.

Each academic year, I encounter a few personal examples of cheating in my own classes or in the classes of friends and colleagues. That this is an unfortunate and unpleasant feature of academic life is a given. There has, however, been a significant change in this area recently. In talking with students who have been caught turning in plagiarized papers (or papers written by others), I have noticed that the primary reason that they are upset is that they have been detected. This reaction is not so unusual. What is alarming, however, is that many of these students appear to view their "apprehension" as an unfortunate and inconvenient cost of doing academic business, not unlike a truck driver who is occasionally caught by the highway patrol with an excessive load. I have seen such students attempt to negotiate the sanctions for their indiscretions, much as a businessman attempts to bargain for a commercial advantage.

What is missing, of course, is a recognition of the moral laxity involved in plagiarism or other forms of academic dishonesty. Once again, student attitudes on the ethical level appear to mirror the pattern of misconduct that pervades the university as a whole. To add yet another element to an already dubious situation hardly encourages a serious commitment to excellence in higher education.

My fear is that American universities are doing little to prevent the emergence of a student generation of moral incompetents. I hesitate to use milder language here, because I see daily expressions of this phenomenon in my own classes and in my office conversations with undergraduates. At UCLA, for example, my classes have dealt regularly with the realities and ethical dilemmas of professional life. This is an especially appropriate topic for a student population where well over 75% aspire to professional careers. One of my regular activities in class is to present concrete cases of ethical problems for student discussion. I might ask, for example, what a journalist should do if confronted by a managing editor who requests that a critical story about a local politician be dropped, because it could cause a political and economic backlash to the paper or television station. I make it clear that the managing editor is in the position to have either a positive or negative influence on the journalist's career. Or I might ask students what they would do as lawyers defending an accused rapist. Would they, for example, attempt, through the use of their rhetorical skills, to place the female victim on trial in effect by accusing her of instigating the sexual assault? Would they attempt to dredge up her sexual past if it could assist them in winning the case?

I am dismayed by the majority of student answers to these and similar questions. With rare exceptions, the response is that professionals need to do whatever is necessary to win the case or solve the problem and, most important, to advance up the career ladder. While recognizing that they might not feel very happy about this decision, they always claim that this is nevertheless necessary in the "real" world. With supreme confidence, they assure me that this is what reality is all about. Their view is that ethical inquiry is interesting and even fun in a university classroom, but that it has very little to do with life as it is actually lived.

Although many of the student responses to such questions trouble me because of their content, what is even more dangerous is that their answers are so virtually automatic. Issues in professional ethics are complex and ambiguous, and reasonable men and women can come to opposite conclusions. Too many contemporary university students, however, come to the position of compromise as if it were the modern expression of a Platonic form, eternally true and immutable. They have so internalized the view that one must automatically compromise one's values and capitulate to the arbiters of promotion that no underlying process of moral reasoning and analysis supports the result.

Instead, their decision to compromise is supported by little more than shoddy platitudes and a supposed knowledge of life's realities that is belied by their actual inexperience in the affairs of the world. When I posit a different standard for such ethical decision-making, I am usually labelled as "too idealistic," a curious designation coming from persons eighteen or twenty years my junior. Beyond the silliness of some of their comments lies a far more depressing unwillingness to grapple seriously with ethical issues they will likely encounter a few years hence. The implications for the moral character of education in particular and society in general are hardly exhilarating.

The most poignant feature of student complicity involves their passivity in the face of degrading faculty and administrative treatment. More often than not, students feel hurt and upset when they encounter poor teaching, sloppy advising, and Kafkaesque bureaucratic treatment. They have a sense that they are entitled to a much superior form of professional service. At least intuitively, they understand that a huge gap exists between the educational potential of the university and its daily realities.

As I have mentioned previously, I have seen hundreds of students shortly after they have been victimized by irresponsible teaching or depersonalized responses to reasonable requests. Typically, my advice is to protest, politely but relentlessly, to appropriate university authorities. If there is any hope for change, those in power at all levels of university organization need to be apprised of whatever instructional deficiences and unethical actions exist.

Most students, however, seem to accept their lot with a passive resignation that only allows the unacceptable conduct to continue. When I press for reasons for such inactivity in the face of injustice, I usually hear the stale excuse that nothing can really be done, so why bother at all. Once again, I encounter platitudinous remarks about the nature of reality and of the incapacity of large bureaucracies to change.

Such pessimism may well be accurate in the light of institutional inertia, but it also misses the point. There is moral and emotional value in responding vigorously to bureaucratic wrongs, even if objective success is only marginal or non-existent. Probably the saddest comments I have heard from students consist of remarks like "this is the way it has always been and someday it will be my turn at the top." While I usually counter by arguing that the passivity of the victim reinforces the system as a whole, I find it difficult to contain my sense of despair.

If undergraduate students could overcome their ineffective stoicism, there are ways by which their complicity in educational mediocrity could be significantly reduced. Above all, they should be encouraged to understand the fundamental deficiences of the modern American research university. To do so requires a much more serious commitment to intellectual development than presently exists. Such a commitment, in turn, demands a far more rigorous effort than the mere diligence required to obtain good grades.

A more serious analytic foundation is necessary if there are to be any effective student efforts to address some of the failures of American higher education. Such a foundation requires hard work and a willingness to transcend the understandable but vague dissatisfactions that often characterize student life. Serious thought and analysis could in turn generate systematic action, as it sometimes has in the past. Although not all student actions directed against educational inadequacies during the activist 1960's were effective or even intelligent, some were both effective and intelligent. If the university is to be more than a sophisticated socialization agent, students must stop being guilty of complicity and start being active protagonists for progressive change.

Despite the criticisms I have expressed in this chapter, I believe that contemporary university students have an enormous capacity to proceed in this direction. They need, I believe, to seek longer range objectives. They should work to alter the present priority scheme that encourages narrow and orthodox research at the expense of a more rational and beneficial system of undergraduate education. The aim, clearly, should not be to destroy the research mission of the institution, but rather to create a more balanced arrangement that will benefit students, faculty, and the public alike.

Most importantly of all, students should demand as much of themselves as they demand of the faculty and the administration. It would be fruitless indeed to elevate the value of undergraduate education if large numbers of students remain selfish, apathetic, and intellectually myopic. A renewed commitment to educational rigor at all levels of university affairs is the best and most durable antidote to educational mediocrity.

NOTES

1. Jose Ortega y Gasset, *Mission of the University* (New York: Norton, 1966), p.79.

CHAPTER 7

Tilting at Windmills: Educational Reform in the Modern Research University

During the mid-1960's, a time of enormous political ferment and dramatic educational experimentation, many students, professors, and social analysts prophesized that American higher education would be progressively and permanently transformed. Many, caught up in the exciting spirit of the times, were certain that their efforts at educational reform had to succeed, because they were morally superior to the traditional programs and priorities they sought to supplant. Rarely in American history has there been a similar mood of hopefulness and optimism.

There were, however, some more skeptical and pessimistic voices. Writing at the same time, John Gardner expressed some more depressing thoughts about the prospects for serious institutional change in large research universities:

> Almost any proposal for major innovation in the universities today runs head on into the opposition of powerful vested interests. And the problem is compounded by the fact that all of us who have grown up in the academic world are skilled in identifying our vested interests with the Good, the True, and the Beautiful, so that the attack on them is by definition subversive.

> Nowhere can the operation of vested interests be more clearly seen than in the functioning of university departments. The average department holds on like grim death to its piece of intellectual terrain. It teaches its neophytes a jealous devotion to the boundaries of the field. It assesses the significance of intellectual questions by the extent to which they can be answered

153

without going outside the sacred territory. Such vested interests effectively block most efforts to reform undergraduate education.[1]

Gardner spoke with the advantage of great personal experience. A long-standing insider in university affairs, he realized that deeply ingrained attitudes could combine with powerful institutional inertia to defeat even the most enthusiastic and highly publicized challenges to the educational status quo. Although it is distressing for me to admit, intellectual candor requires a judgment that Mr. Gardner's comments have stood the test of time and are in fact far more accurate than the wishful remarks of his more hopeful counterparts of the 1960's.

There have, of course, been some impressive efforts at curricular change in American institutions of higher learning. Several schools have responded to the positive educational ferment of the 1960's by establishing and supporting outstanding alternatives to the standard disciplinary fare.[2] A few institutions such as Hampshire College and Evergreen State College have even totally eliminated traditional educational structures in favor of a complete commitment to interdisciplinary education. The spirit of the 1960's has doubtless had some beneficial effects upon the course and direction of contemporary academic life, even in universities most resistant to major change. Many of today's innovations that seek more integrative approaches to knowledge and that explore the political, social, and ethical implications of academic work would never have been initiated without the agitation of the 1960's and early 1970's. At the same time, Gardner's gloomy remarks about the problems and prospects of academic change are still disturbingly relevant to most large, prestigious universities where research and graduate training dwarf all other institutional functions.

As I indicated in Chapter 1, I believe that many of the educational problems identified during the excitement of the 1960's remain unsolved. Indeed, as I noted, many of the daily problems in teaching, advising, and administrative treatment have worsened. Where there is little university incentive to change, drastic cutbacks in funds compounded by an even more cumbersome bureaucracy make this result inevitable. While a few of the educational reforms of a decade or more ago have managed to survive or even prosper, many more have long since gone the way of the dinosaur. Far too many of the interdisciplinary and other innovative programs established in research universities were intended to self-destruct. Their major purpose was to serve as palliatives for restless and agitated students and to respond dramatically but inexpensively to legislatures, governing boards, and mass media pressures for instructional reform.

It is useful to assess more closely the longer term implications and consequences of the educational reform movement of the 1960's. What gains have been made, what problems continue to exist, and what kinds of strategies are useful for what kinds of educational reform are vital problems today. The answers have immense implications for the lives of millions of American university students and for the world they will inhabit during the coming century.

The University of California again provides a useful focus for this inquiry. As an institution, it epitomizes the enormous range of problems faced by academic innovators, especially those who seek to create and institutionalize interdisciplinary units as alternatives to traditional academic departments. For many years, its international reputation has been predicated on the quality of its faculty's research and on its recognized excellence as a center for graduate and professional training. These accomplishments are the raison d'etre of research universities, and the University of California has simply exceeded almost all other universities in recognition along such lines.

In the years following the Free Speech Movement at Berkeley (and similar if less publicized eruptions at many of the other campuses), the entire institution came under severe attack by many students, some progressive faculty members, and certain members of the California State Legislature and the Board of Regents of the University of California. These forces condemned the university for failing to address its pressing educational problems. These critics argued persuasively that its research prestige, based as it was on narrow disciplinary accomplishments, defeated the objective of a more desirable and integrative education for undergraduates - one of the central theses of the present book.

In response to this political pressure, the University of California established official commissions and select task forces that attempted to discover the sources of student alienation and educational dissatisfaction. The most notable report to emerge in the post-FSM period was entitled "Education at Berkeley," authored primarily by Professor Charles Muscatine of the Department of English on the Berkeley campus. This report urged a variety of reforms and some recommendations (but not, significantly, strong *demands* or mandated *requirements*) that teaching be made more relevant in determinations of faculty promotion and tenure. Sincere and useful as far as it went, the Muscatine Report was all too typical of university documents that attempt to address the problems of inadequate undergraduate education. Promoting mild reform and progressive sentiment, it nevertheless allowed most research-bound professors to ignore its impact and continue to work in accordance with their same inclinations that give rise to profound educational dissatisfaction in the first place.

The University of California did in fact institute some actual curricular change[3] in addition to the usual committee reports and public relations rhetoric. Many of the critics, however, maintained that most of this effort was mere window dressing, especially at Berkeley. Two scholars who investigated this situation at Berkeley as part of a broader inquiry into the politics of educational innovation concurred: "Berkeley is perhaps the prototype among American universities, of frenetic activity, grandiose planning, dramatic pronouncements, and virtually no change."[4]

More than a decade later, the University of California continues to be an outstanding case study for an examination of the severe problems and limited prospects for interdisciplinary and other educational improvements at large, prestigious research universities. The multi-faceted activities of the University of California have a powerful influence in scholarship and education throughout the entire world. The possibilities for reform in this institution therefore have significance far beyond the boundaries of its nine individual campuses. Of course, there are some clear differences among large research universities. Local conditions are always crucial. The presence or absence of faculty members and administrators with educational vision and strong leadership capabilities is a major variable in the prospects for serious and durable educational change. The fortuities of time and place cannot be overemphasized.

Nevertheless, a careful assessment of both the broader barriers and opportunities within the University of California can have implications for similar institutions throughout the country. A useful approach to such an assessment involves an investigation into three interdisciplinary programs at Berkeley and UCLA, the two most powerful units within the University of California system. All three programs are modern innovations that likely would not exist at all had American higher education not exploded in the aftermath of the Free Speech Movement. All three programs have been deemed educationally outstanding in repeated student evaluations. The Berkeley program has been politically beleaguered and for several years even threatened with total elimination. It appears to have survived, however, in a low level, extremely marginal way. The UCLA programs, until very recently, appeared to enjoy some impressive institutional stability. This appearance was deceptive; one of them has been terminated and the other continues to exist on the periphery of the undergraduate curriculum.

Using the Berkeley Division of Interdisciplinary and General Studies and the UCLA Program in Medicine, Law and Human Values and the UCLA Freshman/Sophomore Professional School Seminar Program[5] as comparative examples, it is possible to identify and analyze some major historical, political, financial, and psychological differences between the educational ferment of the 1960's and early 1970's and the present. The analysis of the three University of California cases can be used to draw more general conclusions about the prospects for educational reform in the essentially conservative world of research universities.

The Division of Interdisciplinary and General Studies (DIGS)[6] was created in the wake of the Free Speech Movement. It was one of the results of the numerous reports on improving undergraduate education at Berkeley arising out of the extreme political turmoil of that era. DIGS is a dramatic example of a quality educational program that could never receive full institutional support. Created originally by the College of Letters and Science in 1969, its original charge was to be a place for courses that could not find a home in any one department and for field majors in humanities, natural science, and social science. In its first years, it underwent numerous transformations. There were several changes among the junior faculty and in due course the natural science major was eliminated, a legitimate educational decision given its significant deficiencies. Shortly thereafter, the original emphasis on classical knowledge was reduced and a relatively stable group of faculty members emerged.

Almost from its inception, the social science field major established itself as the dominant unit within the broader Division of Interdisciplinary and General Studies. Its faculty and its particular educational programs soon became the focus of significant controversy at Berkeley. Operating with no more than four or five instructors (some part-time), the major attracted over three hundred students, each of whom devised an individual program combining core courses in social science theory and methodology, historical courses from the ancient and modern eras, and a personal area of concentration that cut across traditional academic disciplinary lines. With careful and detailed assistance from faculty advisors, students combined courses in the program itself with offerings from throughout the College of Letters and Science and other academic units at Berkeley.

DIGS social science students were drawn from a wide diversity of backgrounds. Despite the widespread impression among regular faculty members that DIGS constituted a ghetto for marginal students seeking an easy degree,[7] the level of student performance was high, even by Berkeley standards. Indeed, a significant percentage of DIGS students entered the program precisely because they wanted the challenge of taking personal responsibility for the course and direction of their own educations. They perceived the program as a dramatic alternative to the passive education ordinarily available in traditional departments. Furthermore, a large number of social science majors subsequently entered graduate and professional schools, where many compiled exceptional records.

From the start, DIGS was perceived as encouraging academic superficiality and contributing to a general decline of intellectual standards. Such allegations, however, were largely the defensive reactions of the members of a guild, mindful of their own interests and fearful of change. At Berkeley, these accusations against DIGS were as omnipresent as they were untrue. They were expressed in public and even more often in private conversations in dining rooms, the Faculty Club, office corridors, and other informal social gatherings. Without doubt, DIGS had a "bad press" on the campus and only a handful of prestigious regular faculty members spoke publicly or privately in its defense, a fact made inevitable by a convergence of factors extant at Berkeley in the middle 1970's.

Nevertheless, closer scrutiny of the program in a series of official inquiries and reviews indicated the existence of an enormous gap between the public image and the educational reality. Faculty review committees determined that DIGS was responsible for some outstanding educational contributions at Berkeley. The specific comments of one of the review committees are particularly revealing both about the gap itself and about the broader character of academic life in major American research universities:

> [T]hanks to the devoted service, fine teaching, and superb advising of its Chairman, faculty, and staff, it can now proudly make the claim that it has survived. And it has done something more than survived; it has established its credentials as a serious academic enterprise . . . DIGS has been the prey of rumors of its immediate demise, and even if the reports of its ill health have been erroneous and ill-founded, the suspicion continues to exist that DIGS is not long for this academic world.[8]

The Committee concluded by offering a variety of recommendations that would, if implemented, have strengthened this form of educational change at Berkeley. The report affirmed vigorously that DIGS had earned a place as a permanent part of the continuing undergraduate program on the Berkeley campus. It argued that the program should not be perceived as a pious extra by faculty members who were totally immersed in their departments. It urged the university to support the program as part of a serious commitment to educational pluralism. Most important, it recommended the allocation of modest permanent resources in order to ensure programmatic stability and continuity: "A university as great and varied as this should have a place for a small number of ladder appointments devoted to DIGS . . ."[9]

DIGS faculty and students were understandably elated when this report was presented. For the first time, there was optimism that the program would survive and that its faculty would receive some formal university support for its educational accomplishments. These hopes were quickly dashed. Despite its academic successes and its increasing reputation beyond the Berkeley campus for its interdisciplinary innovations, the program remained in serious political trouble.

The College of Letters and Science declined to provide any permanent resources, a major blow to the highly vulnerable junior faculty in the program. Regardless of their teaching and other academic achievements, neither tenure nor any other form of recognition was available. Repeated attempts to convince the administration to implement the recommendations of the review committee were fruitless. The controversy soon broadened and the issues became a matter of public knowledge. The atmosphere became tense as political battle lines were drawn, with militant students, organized parents, and a few sympathetic politicians on one side, and a resistant administration spearheaded by a strong and hostile Dean on the other.

The sustained political activities of DIGS supporters probably served to preserve its existence if not its essence. At present, its faculty are all part-time appointees who must be reappointed yearly, with no guarantees and no possibility of anything better. Its enrollment has increased, but reports suggest that the character and quality of its students have changed. It may indeed even be a ghetto for marginal students, an ironic manifestation of an institutionally generated self-fulfilling prophecy.

While it is tempting - especially for the faculty and activist students who expended time and emotional energy in constructing and defending the Division of Interdisciplinary and General Studies - to bemoan the fate of a valuable educational program, it is more important to explore the underlying reasons for its difficulties at Berkeley. The results of such analysis can reveal much about the recent history of higher education and can be useful to educational innovators who wish to avoid similar problems in comparable universities.

The major factors in the precarious marginality of DIGS are historical, political, psychological, and institutional. These variables transcend the important but local vicissitudes of power on the Berkeley campus. The failure of DIGS to establish a permanent institutional foothold is a function of its perceived association with 1960's radicalism and its use of confrontation tactics that reminded faculty members and administrators of that troubling era; its threatening implications for the emotions of orthodox professors; its status as a degree-granting unit relying on its own faculty; and the widespread indifference of prestigious research universities in the 1960's and early 1970's towards enrollment and student satisfaction.

From the beginning, the Division of Interdisciplinary and General Studies was tainted by an association with the political ferment at Berkeley and elsewhere during the 1960's. Ironically, its actual educational activities were surprisingly conservative, with a strong emphasis on historical background, an integration of traditional academic fields, and a heavy focus on written and oral communication. Its premises were not unlike those propounded by Robert Hutchins, and its courses used Plato even more than Marx. Nevertheless, most of the program faculty were extremely critical of orthodox social science and of major features of American social and political life. Moreover, the program would never have been established without the Berkeley protests of a few years earlier.

It is important to emphasize that an extremely large percentage of faculty members at Berkeley and elsewhere found the events of the 1960's terrifying and traumatic. Accustomed to the tranquillity of the scholarly calling, these men and women saw those events as an attack on academic order and thus a frontal assault on their most intimate personal values. For many, the 1960's were nothing short of a major life crisis.

Many Berkeley opponents of the DIGS innovations were unable to separate educational experimentation from the broader context of political radicalism. The emotional consequences of many years of building occupations, tear gas,

161

mass arrests, and extreme polarization of opinion were enormous. Antagonists of DIGS often saw it in the same mold as those who would burn buildings and destroy the university. While this attitude was often uncritical and astonishingly inaccurate, it had immense significance for the creation of a hostile campus attitude towards academic experimentation in general. This phenomenon, of course, was hardly confined to the University of California at Berkeley. Professors hold no immunity against irrationality simply because of their expertise in specific academic disciplines.

The Berkeley situation was intensified because most of the DIGS social science instructors had themselves been graduate student supporters and participants in major campus protests such as the FSM. Some continued their commitments to broader social change, even though this was far from their daily concerns as interdisciplinary university teachers. Furthermore, the DIGS controversies themselves, while never violent, were frequently characterized by forceful and articulate student advocacy. Many of the DIGS students were persistent and aggressive, refusing to be intimidated by the pattern of administrative rejections. Clearly, any form of student protest reminded faculty members and administrators of earlier violent demonstrations. In a basic way, therefore, all such advocacy on behalf of DIGS was doomed to failure because of the powerfully negative effects of the entire turbulent decade. It is impossible to overstate the extreme hostility and immense fear of virtually anything that smacked of militant student power. Without exaggeration, many professors at Berkeley were unable to distinguish a firm but non-violent discussion with eight or ten DIGS students from those who would occupy the administration building or march on the Pentagon.

In Chapter 3, I argued that the characters and personalities of university professors had significant implications for university life in general, most often along negative lines. Those elements of defensiveness and personal resentment against those with different academic visions were ubiquitous at Berkeley and contributed to the political problems of the Division of Interdisciplinary and General Studies. In particular, there appeared to be deep, irrational hostility towards DIGS instructors who had developed campus-wide reputations as excellent teachers and advisors. The major and overriding strength of the DIGS social science program was its student-centered perspective. Formal evaluations of the program repeatedly noted that students felt extremely comfortable in talking with DIGS faculty members. This close student-faculty relationship obviously evoked powerful and negative reactions among members of the traditional faculty. As I have maintained, professors are like others who prefer to condemn and destroy what they themselves are unable to match.

A variety of institutional factors also contributed to the beleaguered status of DIGS. An examination of these factors is useful in discovering some significant historical differences between the 1960's and the early and mid 1970's and the present. One important variable was that during much of the DIGS controversies, a relatively stable enrollment base existed. This reality, in turn, had a powerful influence on general campus attitudes, including those about educational innovations. Specifically, this meant that university officials were confident that they would always have substantial numbers of students. Thus, they were confident of a relatively secure funding base. There was - and is - a strong foundation for such attitudes. Regardless of demographic changes in the nation as a whole, Berkeley always receives applications from many thousands of college-age men and women. The very prestige of the Berkeley name encouraged officials to believe that they could avoid the catastrophic implications of declining enrollment for higher education generally throughout the nation.

Such attitudes inevitably influence campus policies and priorities. At Berkeley during the 1960's and much of the 1970's, there was little concern about retaining students. Similarly, there was no systematic institutional commitment to ensure student satisfaction with the quality of undergraduate education. Confident that dissatisfied students could and would be replaced by other students, the university showed general indifference in this realm. The consequences for DIGS were powerful and negative. Arguments about a cost-effective program generating widespread student satisfaction fell on deaf ears. Conversely, the dissatisfaction of DIGS students in response to official hostility to the program had little impact. The view was that Berkeley would always attract first-rate students and that the unhappiness of a few hundred students in a marginal program could be easily ignored or absorbed with minimal trauma.

Another significant institutional factor ensuring the precariousness of the DIGS social science field major was its degree-granting status. Students completing the major were awarded the B.A. in social science and in humanities. Although DIGS students might otherwise have selected majors in such traditional disciplines as political science, history, sociology, economics, and psychology if the field major had not existed, there is no evidence to suggest that they eroded enrollment figures in these departments in any material way. But the existence of a degree-granting interdisciplinary interloper seemed to have immense emotional significance for orthodox academics at Berkeley.

That DIGS could award bachelors degrees from the University of California apparently seemed, in the minds of many, to confer an unacceptable status and legitimacy to the program. In addition, it seemed to place it in direct competition with traditional departments, an image it sought unsuccessfully to avoid. It is important to note also that the program never had a graduate component and therefore no specific mandate to conduct research. Its responsibility instead was nothing more - and nothing less - than the improvement of undergraduate education. In a research university like Berkeley, only educational activity closely associated with research is perceived as fully respectable. The existence of a uniquely undergraduate program offering degrees, therefore, was untenable to many faculty members and administrators.

A closely related factor underlying the shaky status of DIGS was its almost exclusive reliance on its own faculty. Most of its teaching and almost all of its advising were done by persons with no formal affiliations with regular social science and humanities departments on campus. This further exacerbated the estrangement of DIGS from the mainstream of academic affairs. Unfortunately, however, recruitment of regular faculty into DIGS was almost impossible. Since rewards and prestige are derived through research within specific disciplines, there was little incentive for faculty members to participate in a politically suspect interdisciplinary program.

At Berkeley, it was often said that interdisciplinary efforts needed to be rooted in specific academic disciplines.

Opponents of innovation turned this into an almost ritual refrain, a slogan substituting for genuinely serious thought. Although the content of this refrain was questionable, its political implications were clear. More participation from sympathetic senior members of regular departments would have strengthened DIGS' case on the Berkeley campus - and would have begun to address at least some of the educational problems identified by both Clark Kerr and the student protestors at Berkeley and elsewhere. The severe imbalance of research versus educational priorities and the strong disincentives against association with all such programs combined to eliminate that potential.

The climate for educational experimentation at the Los Angeles campus of the University of California is an interesting contrast to the Berkeley experience. While UCLA shares the research orientation of its Berkeley counterpart, there is little of the overriding institutional hostility towards innovative programs. I shall later argue, however, that this difference is ultimately insubstantial. Still, it is useful to examine why such a difference exists and to assess its limited significance for educational change more generally in comparable institutions.

Two UCLA examples give rise to a perspective at least arguably less pessimistic than emerges from DIGS at Berkeley. The UCLA program in Medicine, Law, and Human Values (no longer in existence since July, 1984) and the Freshman/Sophomore Professional School Seminar Program have been limited enterprises with strong academic reputations on campus for more than five years. The first program was designed in order to engage the attention of the professions, professional school students, undergraduates, and the general public in legal and ethical issues in health care. The major objective was to inquire into the underlying value issues found in such controversial topics as abortion, genetic screening and counseling, DNA research, the use of placebos, euthanasia, informed consent, and many related problems. The program sought to identify the perspectives of the major actors in these controversies - doctors, nurses, lawyers, ethicists, the clergy, and so forth. An important goal was to analyze and illuminate the conflicting values and positions and to promote a context for responsible value clarification and decision making in both individual cases and broader public policy areas.

These ends were accomplished through a variety of mechanisms, all of which necessarily cut across the traditional disciplines of the contemporary university. In addition to public forums, conferences, research projects, and bioethics seminars in the Schools of Medicine and Law, program faculty taught a variety of undergraduate courses existing outside of the regular campus departments. The major feature of the undergraduate program was a core course entitled "Medicine, Law, and Society." The program also offered several seminars for small groups of students. Invited faculty from professional schools, the College of Letters and Science, and the wider Los Angeles community offered courses on such topics as Constitutional Issues in Health Care; Ethical Issues in Human Experimentation; the Language of Suicide in Literature; Law, Ethics, and the Mental Health System; Medical Ethics and Public Policy; and many others.

The program was respected at UCLA and elsewhere for its academic stature and accomplishments. Program personnel were regularly invited to regional and national conferences and to serve in various consultant and advisory capacities. These activities, of course, are part of the dominant academic culture in the modern research university. Educationally, Medicine, Law, and Human Values courses were consistently rated highly, with many students reporting that the courses permanently altered their understanding of the intimate relationships between scientific and human values and of the complexities of decision making in medicine and health care.

The other UCLA innovation, the Freshman/Sophomore Professional School Seminar Program, is more specifically directed to improvement in undergraduate education. It is a small, high quality effort designed to meet a variety of instructional needs particularly of lower division students. Drawing on the resources of UCLA's eleven professional schools, faculty members offer seminars that provide the opportunity to learn about the nature of professional work and about the relationships between scholarship, basic research, social problems, and legal and ethical standards of professional life. Seminars are designed to enable students from all fields to understand more fully how professionals' values affect society and the economy. Enrollment in the seminars is generally limited to fifteen or twenty students in order to provide the opportunity for close contact with faculty and fellow students - an urgent necessity on an enormous campus of more than thirty thousand students.

The courses themselves are not small-scale or diluted versions of professional education and training. Neither are they intended to be vocational or pre-professional in nature. Rather, they are broad, interdisciplinary efforts that deal with social, political, or ethical implications of various forms of professional practice. Faculty members combine intellectual breadth and theory with their experiences as practitioners and professional educators.

During the past several years, the program has offered courses such as the Ethics, Art, and Science of Medicine; Law, Literature, and Politics; Interpersonal Violence in America Today; Information, Computers, and Society: The Social Impact of Computerization; Social Change and Social Welfare; Engineering: Its Role and Function in Society; and numerous other topics that cross professional and disciplinary boundaries. The seminars are taken by students on an elective basis. There is no set of core offerings. Instead, topics vary from term to term and year to year. Some faculty members teach regularly in the program while others offer courses on a one-time only basis. The program as a whole is thus a shifting series of interdisciplinary courses oriented to some general thematic concerns.

Like the Program in Medicine, Law, and Human Values, this effort has been well regarded at UCLA. In formal faculty evaluations, the Freshman/Sophomore Professional School Seminar Program has been favorably reviewed. Students have shown unusual enthusiasm for both the quality of instruction and for the breadth and diversity of the seminar topics. Furthermore, program faculty and some university officials have expressed considerable satisfaction about this innovative educational arrangement.

Neither UCLA program, however, could achieve the kind of permanent institutional base comparable to regular academic departments. The Program in Medicine, Law, and Human Values underwent an official review in 1983/84 that resulted in its formal disestablishment.[10] Only remnants of its public programs and undergraduate courses presently remain. These undergraduate offerings are currently organized through the mechanism of the UCLA Council on Educational Development, a unit that sponsors interdisciplinary courses that go beyond the range of traditional academic departments. This entity, one of the token educational reforms generated by the ferment of the 1960's, is likely to endure and continue to present some curricular remains of the defunct Program in Medicine, Law, and Human Values.

The political situation of the Freshman/Sophomore Professional School Seminar Program is only slightly less precarious. It has suffered major financial reducations despite its status as an extremely low-budget operation. In Spring, 1983, at a time of immense budgetary cutbacks, UCLA terminated much of the program's funding by eliminating its key administrative position. A familiar pattern of institutional politics prevailed, a reality all too familiar to academic men and women laboring to improve education for university undergraduates. When money is tight, marginal interdisciplinary programs must compete with powerful academic units for the same soft money keeping the innovative entities afloat. When mice tangle with elephants, the results are relentlessly predictable. Once again, mere academic quality was shown to be insufficient. The real values of the research multiversity surface when the monetary crunch truly arrives. The present status of the program is thus highly tenuous. It may survive in diluted form or fade into oblivion in a few years. It may, on the other hand, enjoy a modest resurgence and sponsor a few more interdisciplinary seminars. Regardless of the ultimate result, its lack of institutional solidity is typical of the fate of educationally innovative programs in the post-war research university.

The major contrast with the fate of DIGS at Berkeley is that there has been little overt hostility directed against either program. This is a more benign attitude that at least theoretically allows for greater educational flexibility at UCLA, at least if modest financial resources are available for experimentation in this domain. There are several reasons for these different attitudes at the two most prestigious campuses of the University of California. Despite their discouraging fates, both UCLA programs operated without many of the burdens faced by DIGS.

Perhaps above all, the UCLA efforts had no connection whatever with the political disorders of the 1960's. They were not specifically created in response to the pressures emanating from the events of that era. That the Program in Medicine, Law, and Human Values and the Freshman/Sophomore Professional School Seminar Programs were not even remotely perceived as associated with 1960's agitation made it potentially easier to survive among academics for whom the entire 1960's was deeply traumatic. The irony is that perceived separation from the specific historical conditions that made such educational experimentation possible is a dominant variable in the institutional standing of given innovations.

Finally, few of the personnel involved in either UCLA programs have been identified in any major sense with 1960's activism. And since neither program engaged in a campus struggle for survival, there has been no rancorous activity or student-based confrontations that could evoke the pathological fears generated by the earlier militancy. One other distinction is significant in this domain. While UCLA had its share of civil disorder, it was rarely as shattering as that of its sister campus in Berkeley. The consequence is that while deeply ingrained fears and memories of the 1960's exist at UCLA, they are probably not as traumatic as they are at Berkeley.

Although both UCLA educational programs had the advantage of no direct association with political and social radicalism, they still operated in a psychological context similar to that of Berkeley and comparable research institutions. This reality may indeed be responsible for the demise of the Program in Medicine, Law, and Human Values. The same types of narrowly based researchers are selected to join the UCLA faculty. Research priorities dominate the campus, as they do throughout the entire University of California system. In fact, as UCLA's prestige and rankings grow, this may ultimately negate its modestly less hostile climate for educational change and experimentation. Despite the presence of some historical and institutional variables more encouraging to innovation, interdisciplinary activity still carries a heavier burden of proof than more orthodox academic enterprises. It still evokes suspicion among traditional academics, if somewhat less openly than before, certainly in the more private councils of daily academic affairs. This condition is likely to persist as long as the patterns of graduate instruction and faculty selection remain the same. John Gardner's distressing observations, once again, are rooted in the basic fabric of contemporary academic existence.

Certain fiscal and demographic realities, either not present or not properly comprehended a decade ago, now operate to keep some of the underlying psychological realities in modest check. The effect is to encourage some modest innovations at UCLA. It is well known that financial conditions have changed drastically since the prosperity of the 1950's and 1960's. Even at prestigious universities, there is considerable anxiety about the decline of various funding sources. Reduced support has already caused severe cutbacks in campus programs and projects. It has also fostered considerable concern about student enrollment and retention, major variables in future competition for scarce resources.

For all its international stature and recognition, UCLA still labors in the shadow of Berkeley, a reality that causes considerable faculty discomfort at the Los Angeles campus. This awkward self-image imposes some limits to its generally vigorous self-confidence. An intriguing consequence is that it appears to be more concerned about its capacity to attract students in the future and to retain these students, many of whom are likely to come from diverse cultural and ethnic backgrounds and to have some serious academic deficiences at the time of matriculation. Enrollment and retention are thus far more important than they were even a few years ago, because nothing less than institutional survival in the first rank is at stake.

This new consciousness has significant implications for both traditional and innovative educational programs. The irony is that tough times *may* promote a more favorable climate for educational efforts generally. The desire to retain students elevates the importance of student satisfaction. When students express approval and enthusiasm for specific academic programs, they cannot be as easily dismissed or ignored as they had earlier been, even during the era of militant agitation. Any greater institutional attention to students works to the advantage of any educational units that evoke positive student responses.

At UCLA, both programs did well in this context. Both drew impressive numbers of students given the limited character of their offerings and the limited structure of a seminar format. More important, they had an enviable and impressive level of consumer satisfaction, a factor that should - but may not - be advantageous in future determinations about funding and survival. In the case of the Medicine, Law, and Human Values Program, what is theoretically possible did not occur, suggesting that this factor may be less important than some educational reformers have come to believe in recent years. Indeed, it is necessary to note that even when external economic and enrollment pressures force university administrators to pay more attention to undergraduate education, such movement is often grudging and reactive.

The two UCLA programs also operated without some of the specific disadvantages faced by the DIGS social science major at Berkeley. Neither UCLA effort offered degrees. Their instructional contributions consisted entirely of optional, elective courses for students who typically major in traditional academic disciplines. Neither program drew students away from established departments. Equally important, neither was even remotely perceived as a competitive element on campus.

The psychological and political ramifications are significant. The UCLA programs were both in fact and in popular perception an adjunct to the primary educational operations on campus. In large universities, an adjunct relationship is far more acceptable. It is less threatening to orthodox academics and easier to support by sympathetic administrators. These practical advantages are underscored when program personnel themselves proclaim their adjunct status in public and in internal university decision making councils.

A closely related factor lending political support (more to the Freshman/Sophomore Professional School Seminar Program and less, obviously, to the Program in Medicine, Law, and Human Values) to the UCLA efforts is that they made extensive use of faculty from traditional schools and departments. This can be a determinative variable in the internal power realities confronting academics seeking to initiate and sustain educational improvements. Educationally and epistemologically, it should make little difference whether faculty members in interdisciplinary or other innovative units are drawn from regular academic departments or whether they are persons for whom superior undergraduate education is a full time responsibility. What should matter is their competence and intellectual rigor. Politically, however, it

171

makes a crucial difference in conservative research universities. It is apparently the only way to establish connections with other campus constituencies and to achieve a basis of support through well-placed protagonists in established departments.

The comparative examples of DIGS at Berkeley and the two programs at UCLA provide powerful insights into the problems and prospects for academic reform at the University of California and similar American universities. What the comparison suggests most strongly is that academic quality and educational excellence are far from adequate in ensuring the survival of such educational programs. In its essence, the large research university is an awkward and inhospitable place for experiments in undergraduate education. The reason is that priorities simply lie elsewhere. It is possible in America to establish a Hampshire College or an Evergreen State, and thus create an environment totally conducive both to interdisciplinary investigation and to the educational needs of undergraduates. It is even possible to establish some small programs with these goals in many research universities throughout the country. At places like Berkeley and UCLA, however, it is possible to initiate such efforts only at the periphery of the dominant operations. The blunt reality is that to a greater or lesser extent, such forms of education will remain a marginal concern at the most prestigious large institutions.

Marginality, however, has many dimensions, some arguably favorable (or at least tolerable), and some clearly catastrophic. It can mean different things in different places, as the Berkeley and UCLA cases seemingly reveal. It can range from precarious existence and debilitating struggles to quiet and largely unbothered survival. For those for whom the latter result is desirable, the comparative California examples provide some lessons on how to achieve the kind of acceptable marginality that best ensures the avoidance of serious institutional conflict.

There are several strategies that can be employed to effect survival or even modest prosperity within a marginal framework. Above all, it is necessary to maintain the highest standards of academic quality. This is a prerequisite to any kind of survival and, in any case, a poor or mediocre effort at instructional improvement has no business surviving. Moreover, if such programs are to endure nationally in significant ways, it is essential for their quality to match or exceed that of more orthodox educational efforts. Moreover, a commitment to the highest academic standards is strategically desirable because it can attract the best students and high levels of satisfaction, sometimes valuable factors in an era of enrollment and retention worries in universities.

Beyond that, it is important that educational reform efforts appear, even twenty years later, to be separate from the agitation and turmoil of the 1960's. Even though that era was instrumental in creating the conditions for educational change, its widespread perception as a tragic interlude in American higher education has powerful political consequences. This reality must be considered carefully in constructing rhetorical and institutional strategies within prestigious research universities.

It is equally obvious that more stable marginality is facilitated when steps are taken to make interdisciplinary and other improvements complementary rather than competitive. Low visibility and repeated assurance of modest ambition are expedients in the psychological and political context of major research universities. Finally, it is useful to reassure traditional faculty and administrators that research priorities are properly dominant and that specific programs designed for undergraduates alone are merely small parts of a pluralistic whole.

These strategies clearly elevate the probabilities that some innovations can survive in large research settings. There is a question, however, that should not be avoided: Is it worth it?

In one sense, there are only deeply personal answers to this question. Those who have spent considerable time and effort in working for educational change in large universities know well how high the personal costs can be. It is not easy to determine whether limited results and marginal status justify the time and emotional expenditures. There is immense frustration in constantly explaining and justifying educational change to university officials and review committees whose perspectives are narrow and departmentally based. This frustration is compounded when the identical process must be repeated with new officials and new committees.

173

It is equally disconcerting to exist in an institutional setting as a second-class citizen. It is no secret that powerful status hierarchies dominate American research universities. Academics choosing to emphasize educational excellence in marginal academic units often evoke attitudes ranging from extreme contempt and hostility to patronizing amusement. All too often, their efforts are dismissed on the ground that they are merely compensating for personal inadequacies in addressing the "real" business of professional scholars.

To compound this unpleasantness, it is often tactically advantageous to reinforce one's marginality through calculated and repeated verbal assurances of modest ambition, adjunct status, and the priority of research over teaching - in short, an expression of inferior standing in the academic structure. Constant pandering to political authority in any organizational setting is unhealthy and debilitating. Once again, the determination of whether such cost is acceptable is intensely personal.

For educators who are sympathetic to the social and political ferment of the 1960's and early 1970's, it is especially distasteful to maintain silence or even disavow such sympathy in favor of political expediency. A still dominant view in major universities is that the 1960's were a fashionable, irrational, and irresponsible aberration now best forgotten. Many faculty members committed to more effective and humane education see that period instead as a more profound and positive era in recent American history. They find it emotionally distressing and intellectually dishonest to disassociate their present educational activities from the moral sources of their professional commitments.

Even "successfully" established alternatives to the standard fare can generate significant personal frustrations. Programs that offer little more than a series of elective intedisciplinary courses such as the UCLA programs can scarcely provide the satisfactions available from more comprehensive educational programs. These latter enterprises encourage greater opportunities for sustained contact with students. They promote more advising, more intensive intellectual collaboration, more possibilities for social interaction, and, indeed, more reciprocal commitments from student populations. Such pervasive involvement in the educational lives of undergraduates is almost intrinsically impossible in limited, adjunct enterprises that merely supplement traditional educational activities in large universities. To eschew, for political or other reasons, the establishment of degree-granting programs is also to eschew the fullest range of professional fulfillment.

A strong burn-out factor exists among academic reformers seeking institutional recognition and legitimacy in prestigious research universities. There is no paucity of embittered, emotionally scarred men and women who have abandoned their commitments to educational change as a result of corrosive institutional struggles. Academic strife is as petty and vicious as any other strife in employment relationships and the personal consequences are just as severe. To have been victimized by academic brutality can have tragic effects on personal and family relationships as well as professional life. The answer to the question of whether it is worth it is of necessity ambiguous. Those who undertake the responsibility of reforming research universities should have strong personalities, thick skins, a high tolerance for frustration, a good sense of humor, a reliable personal support network, and an abiding belief in the tragic life as exemplified in the figure of Sisyphus.

There are, however, more than personal considerations in responding to the question of whether marginal educational reforms in the multiversity are worth the effort. Even under the best scenario at UCLA, for example, both the Program in Medicine, Law, and Human Values and the Freshman/Sophomore Professional School Seminar Program would be fully institutionalized, with permanent status and secure if modest funding each year. Under this arrangement, program faculty and other personnel would at least be free of the debilitating insecurities that often characterize the lives of educational innovators in large universities. They would be able to continue their efforts on behalf of undergraduate education, operating in a benign and tolerant institutional setting dedicated primarily to other objectives.

Therein lies the fundamental problem. Even under the most favorable conditions, the programs at best can provide superior educational services to a few hundred students a year in a university with an enrollment exceeding thirty thousand. This is not, of course, to deny the value of such contact. Having taught in both programs, I know well the tremendous

175

satisfactions of presenting exciting material to outstanding students, some of whose lives have been profoundly changed. Their future work as professionals, moreover, will likely make unusual and progressive contributions in many fields, a fact that reinforces a sense of personal gratification as a university instructor. Nevertheless, the overwhelming majority of UCLA undergraduates would have no contact with either program. In a mass, impersonal environment, in fact, thousands proceed through four or more years of undergraduate work blissfully unaware of even the existence of these or other pleasantly marginal educational alternatives.

University officials and their public relations subordinates, furthermore, would exploit the existence of such programs by proclaiming a substantial commitment to educational pluralism. They would undoubtedly use such programs as recruitment devices in the perennial quest to attract National Merit Scholars and other academically accomplished high school students. They would highlight the educational accomplishments of these secure but marginal enterprises in official documents to the Regents, to the legislature, and to the public. And ironically, it would reinforce the smugness of most university professors, who would be encouraged to do what they are inclined to do, confident that a few other academics, quite inexplicably, are taking care of the needs of undergraduates for a few innovative courses and programs. Curiously, the best scenario could thus underpin the dominant anti-educational priorities of the multiversity by creating an illusion of significant reform. This is the classic byproduct of tokenism, a phenomenon found all too frequently in the social and institutional fabric of American life in the late twentieth century.

In fairness, I should indicate that there is a contrary perspective, held thoughtfully and sincerely by professors for whom educational improvement is a high priority. Working vigorously for the kind of benign marginality that is conceivable (if improbable) at an institution like the University of California, they argue that a steady infusion of integrative programs and curricula will eventually alter the nature of undergraduate education in the American research university. In turn, they assert, the basic priority structure will be transformed to accommodate a more appropriate balance of research and teaching, thus benefitting all university constituents more equitably. This is a view I once held and continue to respect, but now increasingly reject.

Assuming, however, some continuing validity to this posture, certain university arrangements are absolutely necessary. The biggest institutional barrier to participation in educational improvement efforts is the traditional reward structure. Those who work conscientiously in marginal educational programs do so at their own professional peril. Why indeed should people devote time and emotional commitment to innovative education if there are no rewards to be obtained? To create valuable instructional alternatives requires skill, persistence, and intellectual breadth. These alternatives impose demands far beyond those of regular academic units. If the traditional incentives of promotion and tenure (or some reasonable equivalent) are unavailable, few will embark upon the task at all.

As long as no permanent institutional funding is available, ridiculous burdens will be imposed on the faculty courageous enough to become involved. Even those comparatively few academics inclined toward risk-taking will have entirely appropriate second thoughts. At both Berkeley and UCLA, I have spoken to many such men and women, who finally declined to participate in programs they supported in theory. The reasons, of course, were obvious. They asked what was in it for them, and the answer that personal satisfaction would be forthcoming was ultimately inadequate. Unless this institutional barrier is removed, it is absurd to view interdisciplinary and other innovations as anything more than insignificant stepchildren of the university as a whole. The solution is a regular mechanism to reward those who excel in non-traditional educational efforts. Such a mechanism requires the allocation of permanent resources and positions, equivalent to those in the departments of physics, English, astronomy, economics, philosophy, and the like. It is as conceptually simple and as politically difficult as that.

There is, unfortunately, little reason to be hopeful about change as long as research universities care little about their educational mission. What is needed, as I will argue in the final chapter, is the leadership of men and women who have the vision, courage, and power to implement structural changes. Without that, all discussions of educational reform will remain exercises in utopian thought. Until the domination of departmentally centered academic orthodoxy can be modified, education for undergraduates will be an insignificant feature of university life, as it has been, tragically, for more than thirty years.

NOTES

1. John Gardner, *No Easy Victories* (New York: Harper and Row, 1968), pp.97-98.

2. There is an enormous amount of literature on some of these educational experiments. See, for example, William J. Mayville, *Interdisciplinarity: The Mutable Paradigm*, 1978; David Riesman, *On Higher Education* , 1980; Richard M. Jones, *Experiment at Evergreen* , 1981; and Richard M. Jones and Barbara Leigh Smith, editors, *Against the Current*, 1984.

3. For a fuller account of some of these changes, see Chapter 2 of Joseph Fashing and Steven Deutsch, *Academics in Retreat* Albuquerque: University of New Mexico Press, 1971).

4. Ibid., p.33.

5. I am not a disinterested party in this. While I am not detached, I believe my analysis to be objective and accurate. University officials are of course likely to differ in their own accounts and interpretations of the same issues.

6. This unit is now known as the Division of Special Programs, a change imposed during the height of the campus controversy surrounding its struggles for institutional permanence. The earlier designation will be used in the present text.

7. This impression was investigated and dismissed in an official evaluation of the program. See the Report of the Committee on Academic Program in DIGS Field Majors in Humanities and Social Science, University of California, Berkeley, June 3, 1975, p.3.

8. Report presented to the Executive Committee of the College of Letters and Science by the Advisory Committee to the Chairman of DIGS, University of California, Berkeley, 1976, p.1.

9. Ibid., p.3.

10. The decision to discontinue is explained in a memorandum from the Committee to Review the Medicine, Law, and Human Values Program to the Executive Vice Chancellor and the Chair of the Academic Senate, October 20, 1983. The reasoning for the decision is not entirely clear. The Review Committee apparently concluded that the Program was not a "program" within the usual sense of a university program and that it was insufficiently accountable to such traditional entities as the Law School and the Medical School. The Review Committee, of course, might instead have focused more on whether the activities of the Program in Medicine, Law, and Human Values were academically desirable than on whether the Program fit into traditional administrative structures.

CHAPTER 8

An Agenda for Change

Few institutions in America or elsewhere can avoid a major gulf between their articulated purposes and their actual practices. History is replete with examples of organizations and professions with hidden agendas that overwhelm and even defeat their stated goals. It takes little detective work to see some dramatic contemporary manifestations. The American medical system, for example, has aims that often have nothing to do with public health. The medical profession has been justifiably criticized for failing to address the real needs of millions of Americans. Similarly, the legal system in this country often serves purposes and interests that hardly advance the cause of justice. The legal profession too has been properly criticized for advancing professional and pecuniary concerns at the expense of millions of other who are effectively denied adequate legal services.

No institution or profession is immune. Even clergymen sometimes find it difficult to resist the pressures of upper middle class values in our advanced industrial society. There is no paucity of ministers, priests, and rabbis for whom personal advancement and social status far outweigh their commitments to provide spiritual services to their respective constituencies. Career obsessions, molded and fueled by the culture of modern life, are rampant and are fundamentally responsible for the hypocrisies of institutional and personal affairs.

Thus it is no surprise that the contemporary university and the academic profession have fallen in line. Throughout the book, I have shown how academic practices fundamentally defeat the goals of humane education, most particularly for undergraduate students. As it is presently constituted, the modern research institution is educationally mediocre and even disgraceful. For all its inflated rhetoric about intellectual excellence, it is actually dedicated far more to organizational and personal self-aggrandizement. Its most successful activity has been to provide the technical assistance for the smooth operation of advanced capitalism. Its faculty personnel are far more dedicated to serving as intellectual conduits to corporations, trade associations, and federal, state, and local governments than they are to their local student populations. As Robert Engler has perceptively noted, the contemporary uiniversity has "joined the team." It has become, in his words, an "integral member of the chorus celebrating the American way."[1]

A university that has lost its critical edge has also betrayed its public trust. The university should not strive to become an essential component of the existing political and economic system. Rather, the mission of the university should be to educate students to make informed and intelligent decisions about these systems and to produce knowledge that will assist in solving authentic human problems. There is thus a desperate need for change in the operations and goals of modern research institutions. The time has once again come to open public debate on this topic and to stimulate broader discussions about (and participation in) the affairs of the university.

This concluding chapter will therefore focus on a variety of proposals for institutional change. What follows is a series of broad policy recommendations and specific mechanisms by which they can be implemented. These comments and suggestions may well be subject to significant dispute and criticism, a result I would welcome with enthusiasm. We need a renewed process of vigorous public debate on higher education in the United States today. Academics and laypersons alike need to think about what is right, what is wrong, and what is desirable for universities in the final years of the twentieth century. This process has been curiously absent for many years. It should occur naturally and regularly, as part of the responsibilities of an engaged citizenry. It should decidedly not be a grudging response to campus turmoil and student protest. In the 1960's, a series of dramatic events on college and university campuses and in the nation and world gave rise to serious public debate about higher learning. Although the world has changed and campuses are relatively quiescent, the major issues remain. They should not be resolved by passivity, apathy, and default.

Many of the ideas and proposals that follow are not new. There have been critics of the university for many decades. Their ideas not only pre-date the turbulence of the 1960's, but were also highly influential in generating critical educational consciousness during that era. What matters, of course, is the validity and utility of the recommendations rather than their originality. Most important, a serious consideration of these proposals can lead others to evaluate their application to specific university settings and to propose modifications appropriate to their personal goals of improving higher education.

Many critics of the contemporary multiversity spend substantial time on specific proposals and mechanisms for reform. Their efforts typically focus on the university curriculum, the reward structure, the governance scheme, and related features of university affairs. These proposals are often sensible and appropriate, and I shall liberally draw upon many of them later in this chapter. Prerequisite to a consideration of concrete suggestions for institutional change, however, is a broader perspective of the very purposes of the university at the conclusion of the twentieth century. Reform in the absence of a goal or mission misses the point. Above all, university personnel and the general public alike should give much more thought than they do at present to the most basic reasons for the existence of the institution. Only then does it make sense to determine what procedures and policies can move in these directions.

A comprehensive and detailed argument for the mission of the modern university is beyond the scope of the present book. Still, some broad reflections in this direction are useful in assessing the value of the proposals that follow. The present model of the university, defined and implicitly defended by Clark Kerr twenty years ago, is a pluralistic entity with diverse and even contradictory goals and constituencies. For Dr. Kerr, this model precludes any single vision or coherent body of principles that can inform the institution as a whole. As he indicated in *The Uses of the University*, this is an inevitable feature of life in a complex society requiring service from a knowledge industry known as the multiversity.

Stillborn Education

I believe that the university as a social service station is neither inevitable nor desirable. It is time to re-think the intellectual aims of the institution so that a better educational system can be directed towards more humane values. Writing in 1969, five years after the explosion of the Free Speech Movement at Berkeley, Professors Sheldon Wolin and John Schaar offered some extremely thoughtful comments about a more appropriate aim of the university. Their observations are no less relevant in the 1980's:

> The evidence of the destructiveness is all around us ... Modern production has obscured the sun and the stars, and it has also made the cities unlivable ... It ... consumes men's religions and traditions and makes nonsense of their notions of the aims of education. It periodically slays heaps of men in war, and it daily mangles the spirits of millions of others in meaningless labor ... The great intellectual task of the present is the task of rethinking every aspect of technological civilization ... If the universities were to dedicate themselves to this rethinking, then they would not only serve society in the most valuable way possible, but they might even save themselves ...

> The task in part is critical: to examine what technological civilization has done to our language, literature, art, politics, and work. Partly it is retrospective: to expose the historical choices that were made ... in the service of endless growth and power. That study must try to achieve a meaningful assessment of the gains and losses incurred by these choices. Partly it is creative: to reflect upon human history ... in order to acquire the fullest comprehension of the range of human possibilities, and, perhaps, a heightened awareness of the crisis which has estranged us from our humanity and our world.

> We have preferred to call it a focus rather than a curriculum in order to emphasize the urgency of our condition. Technological civilization encompasses and

184

influences all departments of knowledge, hence it is not *a* problem; it is *the* problem.[2]

Many years later, this is still the great task. Yet we are even further away from this focus than we were in the aftermath of the campus rebellions throughout the nation. The human problems identified by Wolin and Schaar have intensified in recent years. The modern university has done even less in assisting policy makers and citizens to address the central issues of human life and civilization. The further immersion of thousands of university professors into scholarly trivia does nothing to generate a serious reflection about those questions of purpose, value, direction, and alternative that are vital for the quality and survival of human existence. Quite the contrary: the present orientation of the modern university deflects attention from these issues by substituting what is personally advantageous for what is intellectually important. This is a problem of enormous magnitude.

A more beneficial goal of the university would be to foster critical intellectual and moral consciousness in both its students and in the general public. Restructuring of university organizational arrangements and internal priorities could be useful in enabling its various constituencies to move in this direction. Unfortunately, such movement would be a major historical departure, for universities over the centuries have almost always been uncritical servants of the social, political, and economic status quo. Serving the dominant social classes and training their technical elites, universities have in reality become part of the problem rather than part of the solution. In the nuclear age, however, the stakes are considerably higher.

What - if anything - can be done to change the historical and present course of academic affairs? A key element in any meaningful change is leadership, a quality often proclaimed in public rhetoric and rarely practiced in actual fact. Leaders are men and women of ideas, vision, and courage who are able to formulate and implement changes and innovations. They anticipate problems, mold policies, and move institutions in directions that will be beneficial for decades to come. In universities, genuine leaders would therefore be people who understand that today's educational programs affect students whose lives and careers will extend well into the twenty first century.

Few are aware, however, of the utter paucity of leadership in contemporary American higher education. Writing on this topic in 1977, Professor Frederick Reif of the University of California at Berkeley described this sad state with unusual candor.[3] He noted that university Deans, Provosts, Chancellors, and Presidents, the ostensible leaders of academic institutions, usually operate as mere administrators and managers. They are consumed with the demanding tasks of keeping the daily functions of university operations going with reasonable facility and efficiency. This is, to be sure, no trivial task in an era of fiscal scarcity, external pressure, and institutional complexity. Daily administration requires enormous energy and skill and it consumes the time of even those who are inclined to think about broader educational and other issues.

But as Reif indicates, mere management is far from adequate. While it can cope with the routine problems if done effectively, it does little to adapt to the new needs and challenges of a complex, technological social order. Equally important, it discourages regular and critical examination of institutional values and operations. Instead, administrators tend to feel successful if they can keep problems contained and ensure that the major constituent elements in the university are relatively content. Over time, conflict resolution becomes an end in itself. The prospects for genuine leadership under these circumstances are modest at best.

This is one of the major reasons why education, beyond the superficial level, is rarely discussed in university councils. Reif is depressingly accurate in concluding that the pronounced lack of leadership is so endemic that change appears unlikely. Still, he argues that it is necessary at least to discuss this problem as vigorously as possible. Key personnel in universities must recognize the profound differences between management and leadership. They must understand that leadership is prerequisite to any intelligent formulation of educational and other institutional alternatives. They must realize, finally, that the present lack of leadership among major university administrators has potentially disastrous implications for both higher education and society.

Reif's suggestion for internal university discussion along these lines should thus be one of the earliest items on the agenda for educational change.

If some academic leaders emerge, as they have occasionally in the past, they must above all have a high level of intellectual vision. This perspective must be broad and rigorous and it must transcend the almost irresistable impulse to advance parochial institutional interests. It is not educational leadership, for example, for UCLA to move from number five to number three in the overall graduate rankings. It would indeed be leadership, however, to assess the shortsightedness of this goal and to have the character to propel the institution in more productive educational directions. In the 1980's and 1990's, real educational leaders will have to resist, not advance, the selfish career interests of university faculty members. The men and women aspiring to genuine academic leadership will be required to gauge and promote the public interest even at the expense of internal dissatisfaction.

At present, university administrators throughout the country must grapple with the tremendous financial problems that have greatly affected every aspect of institutional life. There is no reason to assume that these economic conditions will improve dramatically in the next several years. It is inevitable therefore that educational leaders will have to find creative solutions to fiscal difficulties and to make hard choices about institutional priorities. But there is another dimension to this issue. It is easy to hide behind fiscal problems in order to avoid addressing pressing educational crises. While economic stress poses severe constraints on all aspects of university operations, it is important to realize that not all university problems are monetary. Even more than money, the university needs the will to elevate education to the forefront of university affairs. The task of academic leadership is thus to recognize this reality and to effect change without resorting to the traditional rationalizations of inadequate funds.

There are several specific ways for academic leaders to promote the broader educational goals of Professors Wolin, Schaar, and Reif. One valuable but controversial direction would involve a major devaluation of certain kinds of scholarship in the university. At first glance, such a proposal seems preposterous, for it appears to negate the dominant function of the institution. My goal here, however, is more modest. I do not urge that academic research should be rendered obsolete. Rather, I believe that scholarly values in their present form should give way to a more authentic form of intellectual work. The university and society alike would be better served if the modern university were more committed to a broader intellectual vision and less concerned with narrow scholarly production.

This view requires historical perspective and justification. In his provocative essay "On Academic Delinquency,"[4] Theodore Roszak defined the intellectual enterprise as an act of defiance and risk. Drawing on the example of Diderot and the French *philosophes*, Roszak drew a major distinction between classical intellectualism and modern academic work, which he characterized as safe, petty, cautious, and useful largely for career advancement. In his essay, he urged a rededication to an intellectual perspective that would be a dangerous venture devoted to criticizing, clarifying, dissenting, deriding and exposing. In short, he sought an intellectuality that would educate in the fullest sense of that term. A true intellectual working towards this goal would be involved in a moral crusade to clarify reality so that fellow citizens could apply reason in solving their personal and political problems.

There is indeed an intellectual tradition differing radically from contemporary scholarly concerns. Roszak is correct in urging a return to Enlightenment notions of productive intellectual labor. What might this mean in the modern university? For one thing, it would mean that the ideas of persons like David Bazelon, Walter Kaufmann, and Andrew Hacker, as presented in Chapter 4, would have a far greater status in university affairs. Their common commitment to broad and speculative thought would be a legitimate part of the academic enterprise. It would not necessarily supplant the more precise features of academic research, but it would be institutionally perceived at least as of comparable value. For another thing, it would mean that mental risk and intellectual imagination would be valued as much as technical accuracy and methodological rigor. More than anything, it would infuse undergraduate education with a vigor and spirit that has been missing in research universities for many years.

When Nietzsche observed that the errors of great men were more fruitful than the truths of little men, he meant something far more significant than a critique of his less creative academic counterparts. The broader significance of that assertion is directly relevant to a renewed intellectualism in higher education. For Nietzsche, it was important to stretch one's mind as far as it would go. Sometimes that process would lead to extraordinary and unexpected discoveries. Other times it would lead to foolish mistakes and ridiculous judgments. The latter results were the inevitable price for the former riches, a tariff that he urged should be borne with grace and humor.

Truly effective undergraduate education should involve a similar perspective. Professors should assuredly work to ensure that their students' intellectual products are as accurate, correct, and precise as possible. No one would deliberately foster error and inaccuracy. But more important, faculty members should demand that their students use their minds to their fullest, with a recognition that the results will be spectacularly uneven. This approach, however, will be far more durable, for in due course intelligent people begin to learn and profit from their earlier mistakes. For undergraduates, this form of learning is personal and active. It provides them with a genuine recognition that they have a stake in the very process of intellectual development - a recognition scarcely extant in most large research universities today. Students encouraged to explore their own ideas, even at the risk of grave error, are far more apt to become more fruitful and effective problem solvers throughout their lives. Genuine educational leaders can encourage this result by fostering a broader intellectual consciousness among their faculties, most particularly among those with substantial responsibilities for teaching undergraduates.

As I have argued throughout this book, a serious intellectual perspective must involve a commitment to both interdisciplinary teaching and research. Most complex contemporary and future problems can simply not be addressed by fragmented forms of knowledge and intellectual paradigms determined by past traditions and present administrative expediencies. Repeatedly, I have noted that such issues as nuclear war, energy, medical care, hunger, and comparable topics are themselves interdisciplinary in character. Contemporary students are ill served by universities dedicated, through inertia and lack of leadership, to rigid departmental domination. In order for them to learn to adapt to rapidly changing conditions and circumstances, they need to acquire broad problem-solving skills that intrinsically require an educational perspective that no single field can provide by itself. The parochial concerns of individual disciplines and academic departments impose educational limitations entirely inappropriate to the modern world.

Academic leadership can be tremendously influential in responding to this unacceptable condition of higher learning. Presidents, Vice Chancellors, and Deans with the vision to move along lines suggested earlier by Wolin and Schaar are in a position to foster specific progressive changes in their institutions. It is important to explore some possibilities in this direction. In most universities, Deans or their counterparts administer academic units (usually Colleges of Letters and Sciences and professional schools) consisting exclusively of various departments. Typically, they must make resource and other decisions affecting those academic entities. It would make sense to create and sustain comparable academic units consisting of meritorious interdisciplinary activities and programs, with Deans or other officials of equal stature to those who oversee traditional academic departments. In order to accomplish their research and educational goals successfully, these interdisciplinary units must be furnished with significant resources, including permanent faculty and staff positions.

University leaders can foster such a desirable result in several specific ways. First, they can assume the responsibility of educating their faculties to a better understanding of the intellectual limitations of individual departments alone. Such intellectual leadership can be done with tact and sensitivity, in order to assuage the inevitable fears and insecurities generated by the specter of organizational and personal change. More important, they can generate excitement about participation in new interdisciplinary ventures and they can support faculty involvement with suitable incentives and rewards. Second, academic leaders can make tough and unpopular resource decisions by allocating money and positions to promising interdisciplinary and educational enterprises existing outside the province of traditional departments. When done with appropriate political acumen, such decisions can even generate the respect of those rarely accustomed to internal frustration and defeat. Finally, university leaders can influence changes in graduate education, the incubator of departmentally-based intellectual myopia. By encouraging adjustments in values and operations in this realm, a new generation of more flexible young scholars may indeed emerge. Once again, through a carefully organized strategy of incentives and hard decisions, significant improvement may well be possible. None of these approaches, of course, can offer any guarantee of a better educational universe. The absence of leadership, however, ensures the perpetuation of intellectual fragmentation and educational mediocrity.

One of the most crucial challenges is to reverse the low and declining status of undergraduate education in the large research university. This has been a massive problem for more than thirty years, for reasons I have suggested throughout this book. All of the warnings on this score have gone unheeded. Despite the agitation of the student movement of the 1960's and a veritable mountain of university commission and task force reports, nothing has been able to reverse the tide.

This is a monumental task facing academic leaders because so many university professors and administrators are totally uninterested in the educational needs of undergraduates. In scores of informal conversations over the years at Berkeley and UCLA, I have heard the preference for transforming such institutions exclusively into graduate schools and research units. Without question, thousands of university faculty members would be happier with such an arrangement. Indeed, there is no intrinsic reason why there should not be institutions devoted entirely to such objectives, including those supported by public funds. Research and graduate training are legitimate state-supported functions and a complex university system in particular might properly designate one or two campuses to perform these roles exclusively. The improvement of undergraduate education hardly requires that every university campus be mandated to sponsor an undergraduate curriculum and program.

It would be reasonable, therefore, for some institutions to abandon undergraduate education instead of instituting awkward and ineffective efforts at reform. There is nothing dishonorable about acknowledging a preference for some intellectual activities over others. What *is* dishonorable is to promote a fraudulent perspective to students and to the public. It is not acceptable to receive substantial funding based in part on undergraduate enrollment and then structure university priorities in such a way that education for undergraduate students is fundamentally slighted.

What, then, are some specific directions for university administrators with educational vision and leadership capabilities? As with the need to encourage interdisciplinary enterprises within the university, they can motivate their faculties to have a higher appreciation for education in general and teaching in particular. Effective leaders in all organizations can generate a spirit of common enterprise that infuses all features of corporate existence. This has been done regularly, in fact, in order to stimulate research production. There is every reason to believe that the same could be accomplished in the educational realm. The authors of the 1966 report on "Education at Berkeley" recognized this principle in noting that the quality of education depends on the ethos of the campus. Whether a university promotes a profound concern about teaching has much to do with its ultimate educational stature. Leadership is therefore vital in molding such a campus ethos.

The system of academic rewards must be radically altered if undergraduates are to be properly served and educated. Despite official denials, the modern university rewards orthodox scholarship and often penalizes effective teaching, as I have shown in Chapter 4. Academic leaders must transcend the stale incantation that excellent research guarantees excellent instruction. It may, but it usually does not. Moreover, they must do much more than merely suggest or recommend that teaching should be recognized in faculty promotion. Since the 1960's, such recommendations have been legion, yet virtually everyone involved in research universities knows that the official rhetoric has little or nothing to do with actual practice.

It is not necessary to create new regulations about promotion and tenure standards. All that is required is to implement those criteria that exist in virtually every university in the United States. At the University of California, for example, all promotions to tenured faculty positions require evidence of superior accomplishments in both teaching and research, a standard often ignored with impunity. Academic leaders must insist that their own regulations be followed. They must ensure that the evidence for superior teaching be genuine rather than pro forma. And when the regulations are ignored, they must be prepared to overrule promotion review committees. When unqualified professors are promoted and qualified professors are not, courageous Deans, Vice-Chancellors, and the like must intervene. This harsh and unpopular remedy must be exercised with great discretion, for it inevitably has immense consequences for morale and academic collegiality. But it must be exercised from time to time. Contrary to popular academic belief, good education can be compelled or even coerced. If morality cannot be legislated, behavior can surely be regulated.

Obviously, however, extreme measures involving the exercise of brute power should be kept to a minimum. Academic leaders should realize that men and women on university faculties bring a wide range of strengths and weaknesses to their work. As I indicated near the end of Chapter 4, it may be entirely unrealistic to expect excellence in every facet of academic life. Some professors, no matter how hard they try, will never be outstanding undergraduate teachers. For basic reasons of personality and temperament, they can not feel at ease in the presence of younger students. Some, despite their scholarly productivity, are unable to excel in oral communication or display those qualities of personal character that inspire and motivate undergraduate students. With effort, most of these men and women can develop into competent instructors. When combined with research of first-rate stature, this ought to be adequate for purposes of professional promotion (as it is in actual university practice).

Similarly, there are exceptional teachers who are unable or unlikely to be brilliant researchers. Some want to exercise their unique gifts for imparting knowledge and stimulating thought as the primary focus of their professional lives. Those who write often prefer to produce text books and other educational materials in further pursuit of their commitment to instructional excellence. This too ought to be sufficient for purposes of professional advancement (as it is not in actual university practice). The large research university should have room for men and women of this caliber, particularly when they also reveal adequate records as scholars.

Academic leaders should therefore give careful consideration to a genuine and effective division of labor in the university. Without negating the goals of excellence in both teaching and research, it should be possible to create and implement standards appropriate to individual academic strengths. Within a year or two of initial appointment, it is usually possible to ascertain in which areas professors are likely to excel and in which areas they are likely to be less accomplished. There is no reason why the terms of professional employment cannot be modified in accordance with these findings. This process would not, save for a few extreme cases, require the abandonment of either teaching or research. Rather, the proper balance for individual professors could be mutually determined, to the eventual benefit of all constituencies in the university. It might be, for example, that one professor would be expected to produce a high level and quantity of research and perform satisfactorily as a graduate level teacher. A colleague, however, might conversely be required to perform outstandingly as a teacher in large undergraduate courses, initiate three or four innovative seminars for freshmen and sophomore students, and produce enough research of reasonable quality to ensure his or her scholarly competence. If an organization's success depends on the maximum utilization of its human resources, this arrangement would appear to make considerably more sense than the present, more hypocritical approach.

It is often argued that such a division of labor would inevitably create a large group of second class academic citizens. Whenever I have urged the adoption of this more flexible arrangement for professional development, the response has been that the entire university community would quickly identify those professors promoted "merely" because of their educational efforts. The result, according to this view, would ensure that such men and women could never garner the respect of their research-oriented professorial colleagues. This is less an effective argument against the proposal than it is a sad reflection of dominant university values. In fact, if an educationally progressive campus ethos were present, there would be little talk of second class academic citizenship. The counter-argument assumes that attitudes existing at present must remain in perpetuity. The role of academic leadership, however, is to set an institutional tone that will dissipate those status hierarchies that defeat educational efforts and that debase the very operations of the modern university.

There are several other suggestions that could serve the cause of undergraduate education. In my own work at UCLA during the past few years, for example, I have experimented with the use of professional school faculty members as undergraduate teachers. I have found that with careful selection criteria, these men and women can make a significant contribution to instructional development and improvement. They are able to combine theory and abstract knowledge with their experiences as practitioners and professional educators. When combined with personalities suited to outstanding teaching, this fusion is especially beneficial to undergraduate students who are largely unaware of the dynamics of professional life and of the complex relationships between pure and applied knowledge. The educational contributions of these faculty members are often striking, because they bring an extraordinary enthusiasm to the undergraduate classroom. For many, it represents a magnificent opportunity for professional renewal, a chance for new educational challenges that are profoundly different from the daily obligations of law, medical, management, or library school teaching. Most large universities have large professional school faculties on campus, yet they are rarely used to supplement the traditional offerings in the undergraduate curriculum. Academic leadership, once again, can be useful in mobilizing an extremely valuable resource for the benefit of undergraduate students and regular liberal arts faculty members alike.

A closely related proposal to improve undergraduate education involves the use of practicing professionals as part-time undergraduate teachers. Just as selected professional school faculty members can make splendid contributions in this area, so too can selected doctors, lawyers, clergymen, business executives, public administrators, social workers, engineers, and other professionals. Often, they combine a sound liberal arts background with imaginative educational ideas that would prove highly advantageous to undergraduates. More important, their experience in dealing with diverse groups of people equips them with communication skills often lacking among regular undergraduate teachers. Moreover, they often display a high level of vigor and enthusiasm characteristic of those who are provided with unusual opportunities for professional and personal renewal. It is time for universities to overcome their insular attitudes and elitist prejudices and make effective use of educational resources throughout the community. Again, everyone stands to benefit from a more creative and mature academic perspective along such lines.

In Chapter 5, I wrote about the unprofessional attitudes of regular university faculty members towards their marginal and itinerant colleagues - the men and women on yearly contracts who labor without benefit of academic promotions or the opportunity for even modest employment security. Changes in attitudes and actions regarding these people would also have the effect of improving undergraduate education. When human beings are treated with respect, they are inclined to respond in kind. When they are demoralized, they are inclined to retreat into a state of selfishness that is perfectly understandable under the circumstances. For years, I have talked with many temporary university instructors who have been hurt by callous and cavalier reactions from regular faculty members. Their low morale can be reflected in their own work in the undergraduate classroom. Sometimes they cut corners in their course preparations, sometimes they reduce their contact with their students, and sometimes their own precarious status is reflected in less than inspiring classroom performance. Students quickly learn not to expect much from men and women who are unlikely to be around for long and who are easily identified as an inferior professional class. There is no easy solution to this problem. Economic realities make it inevitable that there will be more university teachers than there are positions. Still, humane treatment, professional respect, and active assistance in helping members of this academic sub-class find other employment would be more ethical and more advantageous to the educational operations of specific campuses.

Especially since the mid-1960's, student involvement in educational decision-making has been touted as a major solution to the problems of undergraduate education. Indeed, ever since the explosions on college and university campuses throughout the country, there has been student participation in institutional governance. Students sit on a variety of academic committees and generally have access to the chief administrators in most universities. For those who care to become involved, there is far greater opportunity than there was fifteen or twenty years ago.

There is no question that active student participation is a strong and positive factor in improving the quality of undergraduate education. When students take an active role in the course and direction of their own educational lives, they are apt to demand more of their instructors and more of themselves. Moreover, their perspective as the primary consumers of educational services is essential in the overall determination of educational policy. And as young men and women not yet committed to the values and limitations of any academic discipline or professional identity, they are in a unique position to provide broad advice and to resist the frequent parochial suggestions encountered in educational decision-making bodies.

There are, however, some obvious limitations to student participation in university governance. Many university faculty members and administrators have resisted the idea of student involvement in policy-making. For them, the idea is almost heretical. They view students as immature junior partners in education and not yet capable of intelligent participation in university affairs. In response to pressure, they have grudgingly allowed students to serve on unimportant committees and have taken care to ensure a token level of participation. Typically, student representatives are assigned to units that are peripheral to the key decision-making bodies on campus, especially those setting budget priorities and making recommendations for faculty selection and retention.

Students themselves occasionally contribute to a diminished value of their own participation in university affairs. Many become as adept as their faculty counterparts in the ways of bureaucratic double-talk. Many learn how to sit for hours in committee meetings and avoid dealing with anything of genuine consequence. Some students, sadly, view their service as a source of resume-padding, making it easier to obtain admission to law schools or other graduate and professional opportunities. Student involvement in academic affairs is thus no panacea.

The antidote to mediocrity, however, is superiority. What is necessary is to get better students with higher motivations involved in more important areas of educational policy-making. Such students are clearly available. At several campuses of the University of California, I have known talented, thoughtful, and ethically engaged undergraduates who have given the most serious consideration to matters of education in the modern university. Often, their insights about higher education are more perceptive than those of most faculty members and university administrators. They are the people whose serious involvement can make real differences in the quality of the instructional services provided to undergraduate students.

Most important,they must be encouraged to participate in decisions affecting the selection and promotion of university faculty members. Students, more than any other constituent element, are in the best position to evaluate teaching effectiveness. They can gauge classroom performance, personal accessibility, and professional commitment to the educational needs of university students. They can determine better than any others whether teachers have really met the standards of instructional excellence.

This suggestion usually evokes nothing short of horror in the minds of orthodox academics in America. They assert that students are incapable of distinguishing between good teachers and flashy entertainers. They maintain that students have insufficient knowledge to know whether course materials are intellectually adequate or not. Most vigorously, faculty opponents of student participation in this area complain that undergraduates are totally unable to judge the scholarly and research accomplishments of present and prospective university professors.

Only the latter objection has serious merit. Students are not in a position to evaluate high level research, for at best they are still apprentice members of the scholarly community. Thus they ought not to have a voice in that aspect of faculty appointment and promotion. The other objections are largely specious, revealing the common insecurities and fears I wrote about in Chapter 3. This is not to suggest, of course, that student judgments are infallible. Like faculty members, they too can make mistakes. Their service on promotion and tenure committees would make it more probable that some faculty men and women, skilled at pandering to student fashion, would make it through the promotion process. This is regrettable but hardly fatal. More important, a strong student voice in this area would reduce the presence of what I have called the darker side of faculty promotion. In Chapter 4, I detailed the events leading to the dismissals of three outstanding teachers on the Berkeley faculty. These junior professors were highly regarded by hundreds of students. If students had been involved in these promotion and tenure decisions, those unfortunate educational results would likely have been reversed.

There is also a powerful need to reduce the suffocating bureaucratic atmosphere characteristic of the contemporary university. I have discussed this phenomenon at some length throughout this book, focusing on its negative educational implications. As usual, there are no easy solutions, for bureaucracy in general has become one of the primary pollutants in modern society. There are limits to proposals for decentralization, because of the very complexity of the multiversity structure. In addition, some administrative empires in university settings are so entrenched that any talk of reduction is hopelessly utopian. Some modest efforts in this direction are possible, however. University administrators and their subordinates can be reminded of their human constituencies. Incentives can be provided to treat people decently and humanely. Selection criteria can be altered so that the administrators in universities are hired and advanced as much for their educational sensitivity as for their managerial competence. Finally and probably most importantly, in a time of declining resources, university leaders should direct those resources towards front-line educational efforts as much as possible. Throughout the country, educational institutions at all levels are top-heavy with management, at times to the point of scandal. There is no reason whatever to add new levels to this already ungovernable arrangement. Where cutbacks are necessary, bureaucratic empires should be early targets for dynamic action.

Another proposal for reform evokes even greater institutional hostility than recommendations for increased student responsibility in educational policy-making. I have come to believe that the public itself must be more vigorously represented in university affairs. This is especially compelling in institutions supported by public funds. Universities perform a multitude of public functions and should therefore be accountable to the people who pay the bills and to their designated representatives. As I have argued in this book, most citizens are scarcely aware of the daily activities and major priorities of most research universities. When parents send their children to Berkeley and UCLA, they naively assume that their educational futures are the central concern of university officials. When they occasionally discover the large disparity between belief and reality, they are often properly incensed.

State legislators frequently share similar reactions when they see that universities and their chief personnel are contemptuous of undergraduate education. I have personally spoken, for example, to several California legislators of both political parties. They are annoyed at university officials who ask for money but who fail to explain in detail what they propose to do with it. These legislators generally want to know whether their expenditures are directed toward appropriate objectives. Some have well founded suspicions about the low priority of undergraduate education and seek to influence university officials to alter their policies and readjust their operations.

Such efforts are met with overwhelming hostility by university officials. The moment the legislature attempts to require a greater institutional commitment to its educational obligations, the cry of academic freedom and political interference is raised. There is, to be sure, a strong historical foundation to these fears. Legislators have sometimes improperly intervened in academic affairs of which they know nothing. They have occasionally meddled in operations totally beyond their competence or their legitimate interests as public officials. More ominously, there is a long and dishonorable history of political interference in universities, where professors of unpopular ideological perspectives are made victims of McCarthy-like repressive crusades.

I am sympathetic, therefore, to the dangers and to the sensitivities of university professors and administrators when it comes to legislative intervention in university affairs. As a university teacher, I have no desire to submit my reading list or classroom procedures for legislative approval. Nor do I intend to submit to any test of political or ideological orthodoxy. This problem however, is somewhat more complex. It seems equally clear that academics are like everyone else in wishing to avoid external regulation. Like doctors, lawyers, and optometrists, they prefer to avoid the glare of formal scrutiny and oversight. They are as adept as others in claiming a special mission and asserting levels of expertise beyond the understanding of the public and its representatives. All public agencies would prefer to receive large expenditures to be used in whatever ways they wish. No one is fond of regulation.

With some unease, I have concluded that legislative bodies should take a much closer look into the present state of public higher education. If there is to be any significant improvement, there must be pressure from above, especially from the sources of financial support. After years of fruitless or marginally successful attempts at internal reform, I realize that progressive forces in the university are inadequate by themselves. There are indeed legislative leaders who combine genuine educational vision with a keen understanding of the delicacies of their position vis-a-vis the university. Their cautious participation could make an important difference.

What are some of the specific directions for public or legislative oversight of university affairs? Most important, more careful inquiry into university priorities will encourage some university officials to pay more attention to undergraduate education, if only for reasons of political and economic expediency. It is not inappropriate for legislators themselves to exert pressure by reminding academic administrators of their own responsibilities towards their student populations. This can be done effectively in formal legislative hearings, official budget negotiation sessions, and in a wide variety of informal contacts between legislative and university representatives.

There are also some concrete ways to promote a higher institutional commitment to educational needs. Appropriate budget language, for example, can mandate that specific expenditures be directed toward particular educational ends. Line items can be established that require the creation of specific interdisciplinary units lying beyond the domain of traditional academic departments. Monies can be appropriated for purposes of instructional development and improvement. Faculty positions can be allocated to universities on condition that a certain percentage of them go to men and women demonstrating superior records as undergraduate teachers. Student participation in educational affairs can be mandated by legislative regulation. Funding can be curtailed when the legislature has convincing evidence of excessive bureaucratic empire-building in university systems. Once again, if values can not be instilled, operations can surely be altered. Such are the realities of life in a democratic society.

Doubtless there are hundreds of other proposals for changes in higher education. I claim no monopoly on ideas that might stimulate thought in this arena. To reiterate what I noted at the outset of this chapter, it is essential to promote active public discourse about the role and direction of universities in American life.

To be candid, I find it difficult to be optimistic that universities will adapt to the changing educational demands of the late twentieth century. Institutional inertia is a powerful source of resistance. As I have indicated throughout the book, most contemporary features of university values and practices only reinforce this conservative tendency. But there is a moral imperative to try to reverse the tide of academic smugness and educational neglect.

The university as a social institution will not wither and die in the absence of structural change. Indeed, it can go on as it has for many decades, with the same priorities that have dominated its existence since the end of World War II. It will continue to produce knowledge and technical personnel for the powerful forces of the American economy. It will sponsor football games on Saturday afternoons and generate glossy public relations documents for its alumni and for citizens in general. It will provide honorable employment for upper-middle class men and women of professorial and managerial rank. It will look very good on paper.

But it will also become increasingly irrelevant as an educational force in American life. As they have for more than a decade, corporations will assume many of the instructional functions historically left to colleges and universities. The major dimensions of post-secondary education will pass, largely unnoticed, into the private sector. What will remain for the university will be the domain of scholarly esoterica and the shell but not the substance of the classic liberal arts tradition. For undergraduates, universities will continue to serve as transitional way stations prior to their entry into adult responsibilities. During their four or five years in residence, they will taste a little philosophy, a little history, and a little science. But they will emerge as half-educated, marginally literate human beings barely capable of active public citizenship. That, even more than the present misplaced priorities of the modern research university, would be a tragedy of gigantic proportions.

NOTES

1. Robert Engler, "Social Science and Social Consciousness," in Theodore Roszak, editor, *The Dissenting Academy* (New York: Vintage Books, 1967), p.186.

2. Sheldon Wolin and John Schaar, *The Berkeley Rebellion and Beyond* (New York: New York Review, 1970), pp.116-117.

3. Frederick Reif, "Where are the Leaders in Higher Education?," Chronicle of Higher Education, February 28, 1977, p.32.

4. Theodore Roszak, "On Academic Delinquency," in Theodore Roszak, editor, op. cit., pp.3-42.

INDEX

ABOUT THE AUTHOR

Paul Von Blum has taught for 17 years at the University of California. Although most of his experience has been at UC Berkeley and UCLA, he has also served on the faculty at UC Davis and UC San Diego. He has taught in 9 different departments, professional schools, and other instructional units. He is the author of three previous books: *The Art of Social Conscience* (Universe Books, 1976); *Audrey Preissler: An American Humanist Artist of Our Time* (Helikon, 1980); and *The Critical Vision* (South End Press, 1982). He is the recipient of two Academic Senate Distinguished Teaching Awards: UC Berkeley in 1974 and UCLA in 1986.